TRANSFORMING CHURCHES

IN PASTORAL TRANSITION

REGGIE OGEA & STEVE ECHOLS

THE JIM HENRY LEADERSHIP INSTITUTE AT
NEW ORLEANS BAPTIST THEOLOGICAL SEMINARY AND LEAVELL COLLEGE

Transforming Churches

ISBN: 979-8-218-94616-6

What Others Are Saying About
Transforming Churches in Pastoral Change

"Even though persons on a pastor search committee love the Lord, love the church and have been entrusted to search for the next pastor, many have not served before. An interim pastor can systematically and carefully guide them through this process. This book describes the opportunity churches have during a pastoral transition period to keep the ministry moving forward, regardless of church size or reason for the pastor leaving."

Ray Swift
Pastoral Leadership Ministry Team Director
Louisiana Baptists

"The transitional period between one pastor's departure and another's arrival is both critical and strategic for a church family. This calls for churches to be highly-intentional and spiritually-prepared for the season. Dr. Ogea and Dr. Echols have produced a genuine gift for those who provide leadership during this critical period of a church's life. Their extensive experience gives them a perspective that few others have and makes this work an indispensable resource for both the local church and the interim pastor."

Shawn Parker
Executive Director-Treasurer
Mississippi Baptists

"Dr. Echols and Dr. Ogea have provided an invaluable resource with a clear pathway how to navigate pastoral transitions. It is rare to find a book that combines academic research and practical experience with such excellence as does *Transforming Church in Pastoral Transition.* Highly recommend!"

Jake Roudkovski
Professor of Evangelism and Pastoral Leadership
New Orleans Baptist Theological Seminary

"This new handbook compiled by Dr. Reggie Ogea and Dr. Steve Echols for churches experiencing pastoral transition and those who help lead churches during their critical seasons of pastoral transition is "resource gold!" You will not find a more practical and comprehensive guide to "navigate the waters" of pastoral transition than this one! Written by two of the most experienced interim pastors in the Southern Baptist Convention, this book gives you all the tools that you need to assist a church while it is searching for its next pastor and to lead a church to make necessary transformative changes during the interim period to get ready for its next pastor. The extensive Appendixes of assessments, surveys, profiles, questionnaires, sample sermons, etc., are worth the price of the book! If your church is experiencing pastoral transition or you are an interim pastor leading a church through pastoral transition, you need this book!"

Preston Nix
Professor of Evangelism and Evangelistic Preaching
New Orleans Baptist Theological Seminary

"Few things can change the trajectory of a church faster and more significantly than pastoral transition. In a day when the SBC is beginning to experience a shortage of a pastoral candidates, what happens following a leadership transition is more important than ever. Steve Echols and Reggie Ogea are supremely qualified to take on this topic. Both have spent a lifetime in pastoral ministry and served every kind of church Southern Baptists have, during times of transition smooth or stormy. I highly recommend this excellent work for church leaders and for pastors preparing to leave a church or preparing to start a new chapter in ministry. You won't find a better resource for churches facing a challenge every church faces eventually."

Chuck Kelley
President Emeritus, Distinguished Research Professor of Evangelism,
New Orleans Baptist Theological Seminary

"Few things in the life of a church are as important as a pastoral transition. With the publication of this significant work by Reggie Ogea and Steve Echols, help is on the way. These men are experienced professionals who help make this difficult process a meaningful and enriching experience for the church."

Waylon Bailey
Senior Pastor
First Baptist Church, Covington, LA

"I love the account in Joshua 3:4, when Joshua's officers instruct the people of God on how to move "since you have never been this way before." As Dr. Ogea and Dr. Echols advise in this book, no two pastor searches are the same. Every interim pastor, pastor search committee, and church waiting on God's next pastor will find themselves having never been this way before. But take heart—building on their vast experience serving as interim pastors, Ogea and Echols offer insightful, godly, and wise counsel on how to move forward in the pastor search process and become even more healthy as a church along the way."

Steve Horn
Executive Director
Louisiana Baptists

"*Transforming Churches in Pastoral Transition* is an essential guide for any congregation navigating the delicate and often uncertain season between pastors. With clarity and deep pastoral insight, this book provides both the practical tools and spiritual perspective needed to turn a vulnerable time into a powerful opportunity for renewal. Every church leader, search committee, and interim pastor will benefit from its "do's and don'ts," biblical guidance, and preparation for what God can do in seasons of change. This is not just a manual for surviving transition—it's a roadmap for doing the right things—the right way to ensure stability and continued ministry impact for your church."

W. Thomas Hammond, Jr.
Executive Director
Georgia Baptists

"*Transforming Churches in Pastoral Transition* is a comprehensive blueprint leading any church to greater health during a leadership change. With upwards of 25% of all Southern Baptist churches being pastor-less at any given moment, this excellent work by Dr. Steve Echols and Dr. Reggie Ogea comes just in the nick of time."

Randy Davis
Executive Director
Tennessee Baptists

"Steve Echols and Reggie Ogea offer churches a rare treasure in their book, *Transforming Churches in Pastoral Transition*. Drawing on decades of ministry to local churches, they provide a wise and strategic leadership plan to help interim pastors and Pastor Search Committees navigate a healthy transition from a pastor's departure to the successful welcome of a new one. I have known both writers for forty years. I have rejoiced to watch them live out a passion to glorify Christ through His church. They have maintained a sterling standard of effective leadership and have endeavored to serve with humility and integrity. They know the landscape of Southern Baptist churches. Read this book for instruction and edification. Moreover, apply its principles to help your church prepare for a God-honoring future."

Dean Register
Founding Pastor
Crosspoint Church, Hattiesburg, MS

Transforming Churches

Table of Contents

Acknowledgements

Reggie Ogea

To: Vicki, my first true love, my lifelong marriage and ministry partner, my closest friend, and my inspiration. Thanks for walking beside me from the very beginning of our journey together. Your strength, your encouragement, your resiliency, and your overcoming spirit motivated me to the highest excellence in our marriage, our parenting, and our grandparenting.

To: Steve Echols, trustworthy friend, resilient pastor, and steadfast administrator. Thanks for joining me in this writing project. Hopefully, our collaborative experience will be useful and helpful.

To: Dorothy and Randy Cox, committed Christians and faithful members of First Baptist Church, Baton Rouge, LA, whose generous gift made the publishing of Transforming Churches possible.

To: Dr. Chuck Kelley, President Emeritus and Dr. Jaime Dew, President of New Orleans Baptist Theological Seminary. Dr. Kelley, thanks for enabling me with the role of Professor of Leadership and Pastoral ministry. Dr. Dew, thanks for honoring me with the role of Director, Jim Henry Leadership Institute.

To: Dr. Jim Henry, friend, mentor, and legacy example. Thanks for being the inspiration for the Jim Henry Leadership Institute.
To: The twenty-one churches that have allowed me to serve either as youth minister, pastor, and interim pastor. The ministry experiences gleaned from these churches provided the foundational insights shared in this book.

Transforming Churches

Steve Echols

To: Julie, my wonderful wife, the love of my life, who is the greatest supporter any husband has ever had.

To: Reggie Ogea, who has had an exemplary ministry in the pastorate, denominational ministry, and as a professor. I count it a special blessing to have had you as my close friend for 48 years. Thank you for graciously allowing me to have a small part in this work that represents our joint passion.

To: The twenty churches that have allowed me to either be a youth minister, pastor, or interim pastor. It was an honor to serve with you, and you taught me much of the material covered in this book.

↗

INTRODUCTION

PASTORAL TRANSITIONS VARY from church to church: No one size fits all. Some churches experience smooth transitions because of the healthy leadership of the previous pastor, a core group of spiritual mature ministry leaders, an effective organizational structure, and a proven strength of resolving congregational conflict. Even so, healthy churches need encouragement and leadership during their journey between pastors. They need steady encouragement in grieving the loss of a respected and trusted leader, in dealing with the uncertainties of change, in trusting the pastor search process, and in accepting a new pastor whose style and personality may differ from the previous pastor. They need stable leadership in the weekly functions of preaching and worship, in supervision of church staff, in counsel to deacons and key leaders, and in management of conflict eruptions.

As the authors of this resource, at the time of printing, we (Ogea and Echols) offer our experience of completing 29 interim pastor assignments. Both of us settled into this ministry of assisting churches in pastoral transition spanning our tenure as seminary professors and administrators. Both of us brought significant pastoral and denominational experience into our seminary leadership. Our entire ministry experience has occurred in the Southern Baptist denomination. We have served churches in the Southern Baptist Convention, and seminaries and universities as Southern Baptist entities.

Denominationally, Southern Baptist churches maintain a position of congregational governance with individual autonomy. Individual SBC churches choose and select their pastors through a process of utilizing a Pastor Search Committee, elected by the congregation to represent them in the search process. When the PSC determines the next pastoral candidate, the congregation votes to employ the new pastor, usually by recommendation of the PSC, together with the endorsement of the church staff and/or the key church leaders. As individual churches determine their Pastor Search process, they also define their preference for the use of an interim pastor in the pastoral transition time frame.

In a perfect world, all churches in pastoral transition would enjoy smooth transitions. The reality of truth indicates, however, that rough transitions exist in churches as the result of pastoral leadership failures, unhealthy conflicts, and crisis interruptions. Guiding churches through rough transitions calls for a different kind of interim leadership.

Several common factors result in a pastoral vacancy:

1. Retirement. Often, but not always, retirement brings an end to a long-tenured pastorate. When the pastor announces his retirement decision, the length of time between the initial announcement and the future ending date allows for the church leaders to determine a plan of action. Some churches will engage in a plan of pastor succession, which may involve a strategy to select the successor and then allow for a time of "change-over", when the new pastor is employed and works "side-by-side" with the retiring pastor for a determined length of time. After the co-existence of the new pastor and the retiring pastor, the new pastor then assumes the mantle of pastoral leadership. In this example, a pastor succession strategy replaces a pastor search process.

Another example of pastoral transition due to retirement involves the retiring pastor agreeing to remain as pastor until the pastor search process is concluded and a new pastor is called to the church. This kind of arrangement would be successful only if both the retiring pastor and the church enter into an agreement of understanding regarding the role of the retiring pastor during the interim time. Our advice to churches that adopt this strategy is to insist in an agreement of understanding that the retiring pastor NOT be involved in the pastor search process, to allow the Pastor Search Committee the freedom to engage in a non-biased search. Also, this arrangement would necessitate a third-party consultant to train the PSC and serve as an advisor during the search.

A third option involves the church considering a transitional pastor for a period of one-to-two years. Some Southern Baptist State Conventions offer transitional pastor ministry training, utilizing the *Transitional Pastor Ministry Training Manual,*[1] produced by Lifeway Christian Resources of the Southern Baptist Convention. The **Interim Pastor Ministries** organization provides temporary pastors to strengthen churches during pastoral transition for greater effectiveness. They offer training for those interested in being an IPM interim pastor and church assessments to determine a church's transition needs.[2]

A Testimony from Ogea and Echols

We are familiar with the terms "transitional" and "intentional" being associated with interim pastor. Excellent material is available for these prescribed approaches. This book can be a supplement to these methods but also can be helpful for churches that elect not to go through the formal "transitional" or "intentional" programs.

In Part One, we define and describe the functions, goals, and limitations of the interim pastor in the Covenant of Agreement with the church. Regardless of whether the "transitional" and 'intentional" programs are utilized in the formal title of the interim, these are terms of central importance in understanding and capitalizing on the opportunity afforded the church during the interim period.

2. Resignation. When a pastor resigns to occupy another ministry position, the announcement to leave will involve a timeline of transition to the new position. If the pastor resigns to accept a similar position in another church, that timeline can be anywhere from two

1 *Transitional Pastor Ministry: Training Manual.* Revised. Nashville: Lifeway Christian Resources, 2014.

2 www.interimpastors.com

weeks to two months. Some church bylaws require a stated minimum notice of departure. The timeline may be influenced also by other factors: unused vacation or paid time off; employment requirements of a working spouse; or family issues, such as school transfers, a special needs child, moving expenses, real estate decisions, etc. Some resignations involve leaving the local church to transition to another vocational position, such as appointment as a missionary, service in a denominational or academic entity, employment in a non-ministry organization, or a situation of mutual agreement to terminate the pastoral relationship.

3. Termination. A forced termination never occurs without collateral damage, often severe and disruptive. Some forced terminations occur suddenly and trigger immediate congregational conflict. Other forced terminations develop over time, escalating to high levels of conflict intensity. While the specific issues of forced terminations will be contextual and situational, with rare exception, they will involve either leadership failures or moral failures.[3]

In this handbook, we maintain that the time without a senior pastor can be one of opportunity for the church to make important strides in becoming a healthier congregation. This chance for progress differs from a prevalent mindset that pastoral transitions cause regression and the best the congregation can do is hold on to the status quo. Never underestimate the energy that a church and its leaders will expend to maintain the status quo.

The possibility of pastoral transition being a positive season in the life of the church exists because of at least three factors. The most important factor concerns how the change process works in regard to urgency. John Kotter has been a leader in emphasizing how a sense of urgency is a prime mover in creating an atmosphere for change. He notes that complacency is a strong barrier to change, and that even "very, very smart people can be astonishingly complacent in the face of needed change."[4]

---

3 See **Part One** – *A Covenant of Agreement*: Engaging in crisis intervention and conflict resolution.

4 John Kotter, *A Sense of Urgency* (Boston: Harvard Business School Publishing, 2008), p. 22.

A Testimony from Ogea and Echols

We have observed how very capable and committed leaders in the congregation can become remarkably complacent. However, we maintain in our experience that losing a pastor can be the stimulus to bring recognition for needed change. The absence of a pastor can awaken the congregation to how much they depend on good leadership and expose weaknesses that had been ignored or unapparent. With the diminished number of qualified pastoral candidates and increasing length of time that churches are encountering before a new pastor comes, a sense of urgency to see positive change can develop. The interim pastor can further this urgency through leadership both in and out of the pulpit.

Another factor in pastoral transition being a time for improvement in church health is the "out of town expert with a brief case" syndrome. Common observation reveals that the response of members of a congregation to an outside voice can be more positive than opinions they hear from internal sources. One long-tenured ministerial staff member remarked that he was amazed at how changes that neither he nor the previous long-tenured pastor had been able to bring about were accomplished during the interim. He noted, *"they would not listen to me or the previous pastor, but they listened to you. There was no way that I or the senior pastor could have pulled off the changes we have seen."* A new voice, especially one church members perceive as non-biased and experienced, can bring an opportunity for change. This effect is especially true if the interim pastor has the credentials that the congregation accepts as making him highly qualified.

A third factor influencing change during a pastoral transition is what Lyle Schaller referred to as "disruptive occurrences", when a significant new factor upsets normal processes resulting in an "unfreezing" of entrenched congregational patterns.[5] These disruptive occurrences can be internal or external, quick or gradual. Few occurrences can alter the leadership structure of a congregation like the

---

5 Lyle Schaller, *The Change Agent* (Nashville: Abingdon Press, 1972), p. 86.

loss of a pastor. Suddenly, the manner in which the church operates can be very different. We believe that stating clearly upfront functions and responsibilities, the interim pastor can thaw the present status quo and help precipitate change.

A Testimony from Ogea and Echols

How much progress the church can make will be determined greatly by how the previous pastor departed and in what condition he left the congregation. Nonetheless, regardless of how negative the initial situation may be, we believe that God can work in amazing ways through an interim pastor who creates intentionally a positive expectation for the interim season.

↗ ↗ ↗

Why Our Book is Different

1. Written from the perspective and experience of two interim pastors (29 Interims completed).
2. Written for those who serve churches as interim pastors and for churches who determine to utilize an interim pastor in their pastoral transition.
3. Written from a strategic leadership vantage point regarding plan and process.
4. Written as a resource for church leaders and Pastor Search Committees who are faced with a pastoral transition in a church experiencing plateau and decline.
5. Written for churches who desire and decide to focus intentionally on church revitalization and turnaround during the pastoral transition.
6. Contains testimonies and cautions from the authors.
7. Includes numerous appendices to assist Pastor Search Committees and interim pastors, including sample sermons.

↗

PART ONE

Before the Journey Begins: The Initial Conversation; A Covenant of Agreement; Positioning for a Strong Start

FROM OUR EXPERIENCE, churches cluster in several categories:

Option One

Some churches predetermine that the current church staff and/or key leaders will handle all of the pastoral leadership roles, thus eliminating the need for an interim pastor. Larger churches who choose this option may utilize a church staff member or members to handle the preaching responsibilities, or schedule guest preachers, or a combination of both. Smaller churches who choose this option will schedule guest preachers for the duration of the pastoral transition period. Once the preaching strategy is settled, the other pastoral leadership functions will then be leveraged among the church staff and/or key leaders.

A Word of Caution

While this option leverages the functional elements of pastoral ministry, the distinctive leadership function of a senior pastor is left unfilled. For example, addressing endemic problems can be difficult in the absence of senior pastor leadership. In one of our more recent pastoral transition situations, the church staff admitted that some proposed changes were received positively from the congregation because they originated with the interim pastor that would have been met with resistance had they originated from within the church staff, as we noted in the previously mentioned case in the Echols' interim.

More than just dealing with problems or addressing change issues, an opportunity for the church to go through an envisioning process is much less likely to happen in the absence of pastoral leadership during a pastoral transition.[1] Furthermore, this option robs the church of continuity in the pulpit for the duration of the pastoral transition.

Option Two

Other churches will engage an interim pastor with the primary responsibility of handling the preaching duties and utilizing the church staff to leverage the functional elements of pastoral ministry, as stated in Option One above. The church may seek the counsel of the "interim preacher" in other areas of leadership function, but as a "needs only" situation. While exceptions do exist, this "interim preacher" is not involved with the pastor search committee (PSC) or the pastor search process.

A Word of Caution

For many churches this choice is driven by cost consideration, especially if the church is not meeting its budget. While this option sounds reasonable, leadership vacuums can occur

1 See the discussion on establishing the church's future vision in the section *Addressing the Current Situation*, **Part Two: The First 60 Days**.

during a pastoral transition where the distinctive leadership function of a senior pastor is missing (even in healthy churches with solid financial stability). A strong personality, or a group of strong personalities, can seize control and move the church toward an unhealthy agenda. Small problems or disagreements can escalate into crises, or lead to factions and power struggles.[2]

Option Three

The third option involves the church selecting and calling an interim pastor who will not only handle the preaching/worship leadership function, but who will also provide leadership and limited pastoral care. We believe this option provides the best results for churches in pastoral transition, regardless of the size of the church. Our book is written from this vantage point, and thus, our initial conversation with churches starts here.

↗ ↗ ↗

The Initial Conversation

If a church chooses to engage the pastoral transition period utilizing the first two options, or variations thereof, then this initial conversation is short. If a church is open to the third option, and/or has determined this course of action, then we move forward to prayerfully consider the invitation. Very early in this conversation, we seek to determine a "real sense of urgency" – the first step in Kotter's eight-step change framework first articulated in his ground-breaking book *Leading Change*.[3] After extensive interviews with business leaders and research involving over 100 companies and organizations, Kotter concluded that "creating a high

---

2 Tom Harris, *Soaring Between Pastors* (Wheaton, IL: Big Snowy Media, 2021), p, 20.

3 John Kotter, *Leading Change* (Boston: Harvard Business Review Press, 1996). Kotter expanded his eight-step change process in *A Heart of Change* (Boston: Harvard Business Review Press, 2002) and *Our Iceberg is Melting* (New York: St. Martin's Press, 2005).

enough sense of urgency with a large enough group of people" is the key component in organizational change.[4]

In the past twenty years, the field of church revitalization produced excellent resources which focus on strategies and processes of congregational change. Many of these resources utilize and contextualize the business and organizational models of change championed by Kotter and other leaders like him. A few of these resources, like Thom Rainer's *Who Moved My Pulpit* and Gary McIntosh's *There's Hope for Your Church*, define a sense of urgency as a critical issue in church revitalization. We (Ogea and Echols) believe that until and unless a church experiencing plateau and decline embraces a real sense of urgency, then the search for the next pastor most often will not result in a leader committed to revitalization.

As stated in the introduction, this book is written as a resource for pastor search committees and church leaders who are faced with a pastoral transition in a church experiencing plateau and decline. While we have served churches in a healthy posture of pastoral transition, most of our interim pastor situations occur in churches who desire and decide to focus intentionally on church revitalization and turnaround during the pastoral transition. With positive outcomes, we believe that a viable model of church revitalization involves the search and selection of a pastor who desires to lead a church in turnaround, through a commitment to long tenure and the strategic leadership competencies and proficiencies required for revitalization. For this to happen, intentional agreements and covenants must be settled between the potential interim pastor and the church.

↗ ↗ ↗

A Covenant of Agreement

Before we will agree to serve as interim pastor, we engage in a discussion regarding a covenant of agreement, which involves both the relationship and agreement of the interim pastor to the church and

4 John Kotter, *A Sense of Urgency* (Boston, Harvard Business Press, 2008), vii.

the relationship and agreement of the church to the interim pastor. The agreement of the church to the interim pastor should include compensation, work schedule, and absences. We request that this covenant of agreement be approved by whoever is responsible for decision-making, and shared with the entire congregation.[5]

The covenant of agreement must include the areas of function which the interim pastor cannot fulfill, usually because of time and distance constraints. Limitations regarding weddings and funerals, including grief ministry; pastoral care responsibilities, such as hospital visitation; and weekly church staff meetings must be addressed in the agreement. Most of these responsibilities can be delegated within the church staff, deacons, and ministry leaders. Since Sundays demand the interim pastor's primary focus, the church's organizational structure must be adjusted to allow for Sunday afternoons and evening meetings and interactions. If a Wednesday evening is involved in the interim pastor's schedule, then some of these functions can be leveraged between Sundays and Wednesdays. In all pastoral transition situations, the church staff, deacons and ministry leaders must be willing to "step up and do more" during the transition time frame to keep the church moving forward.

As part of the covenant, in addition to the visioning process, the interim pastor will emphasize the mobilization of as many of the congregation as possible to do ministry. It is important to enlist the maximum number of church members to get involved in the ministry. The deacons can be of great assistance in compiling a list of priority ministries that need to be ongoing during the interim.

The covenant of agreement clarifies our three key functions as the interim pastor.

1. Serve as the preacher and worship leader for the Sunday AM and/or PM services, and Wednesday evenings when possible or available. When the distance prohibits both Sundays and Wednesdays, then the Sunday preaching and worship planning engagement become primary. Even though we confirm emphatically that we are not interested in just being the interim preacher, preaching

---

5 See **Appendix A** for a sample *Covenant of Agreement*. In addition to the duties and responsibilities of the interim pastor and the church, a functional understanding would involve a three-to-six-month evaluation to discuss the effectiveness and efficiency of the covenant of agreement.

and worship leadership provide the most effective function of our relationship with the church during the period of pastoral transition.

As we will discuss in Part Two, affirming and reaffirming the church's purpose and profile must be confronted within the first 90 days of interim pastor tenure. We begin immediately to address the church's current situation and the immediate needs throughout the first few weeks of Sunday sermons. If distance and time permits involvement in midweek meetings, these Bible studies and discussions enhance the Sunday sermons.

2. Provide leadership, as needed or requested, to church staff, deacons, the PSC, and ministry organizations/ committees. Although our weekly involvement as interim pastor is limited and reserved, we believe that this responsibility builds trust and credibility during the pastoral transition. Especially in churches where pastoral leadership failure defines the critical reason for the departure of the previous pastor, or pastors, building trust by the interim pastor should be the main focus in the first 90 days.[6]

Providing leadership to the church staff, deacons, the PSC, and the ministry organizations/committees is one of the critical issues in churches that do not engage an interim pastor, especially in medium-sized churches and large churches with multi-staff and well-defined organizational structure. If a leader in the transition period does not replace the departed leader, then the questions arise: Who supervises the staff? Who do the deacons and church leaders turn to for counsel and advice? Who provides wisdom and structure to the pastor search process? Some churches can address these issues from within the organization with healthy results. However, it is our experience that too many unintended conflicts and problems can sabotage the pastoral transition in the absence of an interim pastor.

Leading and supervising the church staff addresses several critical issues that can arise during a pastoral transition. In the absence of an "overseer," opportunities can develop subtly for staff members to stray

---

6 Building credibility and trust when credibility and trust has been fractured by the previous pastor, or pastors, allows the interim pastor an opportunity to set an example regarding the development of a new pastor profile, described in **Part Three**. A key component of the new pastor profile should state the importance of pastoral tenure. No one size fits all, but it is our conviction that revitalization and turnaround require a five-to-ten-year commitment by the new pastor.

from their established "lanes of ministry." Leadership oversight from the interim pastor enables assigned ministry functions to continue forward. Additionally, our experience proves that this oversight may thwart any attempts from within the congregation to enable dissatisfaction with a particular staff member or discontent with a ministry direction.

Another potential issue may arise if a staff member positions to become the next pastor. This possibility may be initiated by the staff member or from pressure within the congregational constituency. The potential danger of moving too fast with this possibility creates friction, which threatens congregational unity, and usurps the pastor search process. When a church staff member positions to become the next pastor, unhealthy congregational alliances and resistance can result in unintended congregational conflict. Pressure on the pastor search process may force aborting an open candidate search to consider only the interested staff member.

A Testimony from Ogea and Echols

In some contexts, a church staff member is a legitimate pastoral candidate. When that situation occurs, we counsel the PSC to address it early and openly to eliminate ongoing disruption. In a situation where the church staff member would not be considered a viable pastoral candidate, the potential danger posed following the decision may result in the staff member deciding not to stay at the church and seeking another place of service.

A Testimony from Echols

Of the 12 interims that I have done, on four occasions the issue has arisen concerning a ministerial staff person becoming the senior pastor. In only one case did this actually occur. Of the other three, one declined the offer, and the other two withdrew when they realized they did not have the support of the committee. In all of these cases, the work of the interim pastor was key in keeping the situation from becoming very polarizing and divisive.

One key observation is that it is more difficult for an inside candidate to get a very high percentage vote from the congregation concerning becoming the new senior pastor. If the vote is by secret ballot and the church is unified, it is common to see the vote be 90 percent or above. This is because the church trusts the committee, and there is a natural optimism about an outside candidate for which the church has not had a chance to observe any of his faults, unlike an inside candidate. In both cases that I experienced with the committee declining to call the inside candidate, the reasons were that it was difficult to see them transitioning to a new role when the present role had long been established, and the flaws of the inside candidate had been observed.

A Testimony from Ogea

In one pastoral transition situation, eight months elapsed between the time of departure by the previous pastor and my engagement as interim pastor. During those months, a carousel of special-guest preachers paraded Sunday after Sunday. A PSC was elected, and began to consider viable candidates, including one who made it all the way through the vetting process, and would have been presented as the next pastor had he not rescinded his interest. The church staff assumed the weekly pastoral ministries, led by the associate pastor, who positioned himself to be considered as the next pastor. When I arrived as interim pastor, I immediately sensed, after discussions with the PSC and other key leaders, a resistance to the associate pastor becoming the next pastor. Dealing with this issue became a situation of conflict which required immediate intervention.

3. Engage in crisis intervention and conflict resolution. We believe that intentional crisis intervention and conflict resolution should be a key function of the interim pastor. When a pastoral transition occurs, the issues surrounding the transition may introduce situations of conflict or crisis. Residual situations of crisis or conflict can escalate during a pastoral transition. Unplanned and unforeseen situations of crisis and conflict may erupt during the transition, requiring and demanding immediate attention. Most interim pastors can function as "seasoned veterans" in crisis intervention and conflict resolution because of their previous congregational and/or denominational experience. We will address in more detail a plan of action for crisis intervention and conflict resolution in **Part Two: The First 60-days**.

We believe that this function of the interim pastor should be identified in the covenant of agreement, especially in situations of residual or long-term situations of conflict or crisis. Sometimes, residual or long-term conflict or crisis precipitates the need for a steady hand of leadership in pastoral transition. No perfect churches exist – all congregations, even those designated as healthy, contain residual or long-term situations of conflict or crisis. When the initial conversation leads to a covenant of agreement, we often ask, if not already addressed, "What issues or problems exist here, that could be addressed or solved during these days of pastoral transition, that would be a blessing to the next pastor?"[7]

↗ ↗ ↗

Positioning for a Strong Start

When the initial conversation and covenant of agreement converge, the pastoral transition is ready to begin. While all situations are different with regard to start times and timelines, positioning for a strong start is crucial. We advocate for an "in view of a call" Sunday, where the proposed interim pastor preaches in view of a call, followed by a special-called congregational meeting. The responsible organizational committee or ministry team will present the covenant of agreement and a congregational vote is taken. With a positive agreement and acceptance in place, the tenure of the interim pastor begins at the start date agreed upon.

Most churches will announce a special-called congregational meeting for this purpose. The special-called congregational meeting

7 See **Part Two,** *A Plan of Action for Solving Problems, Resolving Conflicts, and Managing Crises.*

may occur immediately following the Sunday "in view of a call" sermon, with the vote taken and the results announced. The interim pastor, now installed, along with his spouse, if present, will stand in front to be greeted by all as a closing ceremony. Some churches may schedule a welcome reception at a later time as a "meet and greet" occasion.

With the "Before the Journey" details now complete, transforming churches in pastoral transition now enters **Part Two: The first 60-days.**

A Testimony from Ogea

In one of my first sermons as interim pastor, I address "How to Get Ready for Your New Pastor." This sermon could be preached on the "in view of a call" weekend, or a prior Sunday of pulpit supply. This sermon takes the church "off guard" as they would expect a sermon like this as one of my last sermons as the new pastor is coming. Utilizing Hebrews 12:1-3 as the biblical text, I ask the church to take three "Looks": "Look Ahead – The Race is Forward;" "Look Within – Examine Your Own Commitment;" and "Look Up – Keep Your Eyes on Jesus."[8] When the new pastor is selected, the last sermon I preach before the new pastor's first arrives is "Ready for Your New Pastor." Utilizing the same biblical text and the same "Looks", I review the journey and commend the church for "Looking Ahead," "Looking Within," and "Looking Up." Sometime within the first month as interim pastor I will address the church's opportunity for revitalization and change in a sermon entitled "A Door Set Open," connecting the church at Philadelphia in Revelation 3 as a case study: "Look, I have placed before you an open door that no one can close because you have but little power; yet you have kept my word and have not denied my name." This text allows for a focus on accepting the reality of the present and activating a hope for the future.[9]

8 See Appendix B: Sermon *"How to Get Ready for Your Next Pastor."*

9 See Appendix C: Sermon *"A Door Set Open."*

↗

PART TWO

The First 60 Days

STARTING WELL IS CRUCIAL to any new beginning, but especially important in a pastoral transition. Many churches experience an "unsettled" and "uncertain" mood as the period of pastoral transition ensues. An urgent function of the interim pastor involves creating an atmosphere of optimism, encouragement, and stability. With the interim pastor positioned as the leader and not just the preacher, three immediate strategic initiatives must be embraced within the first 60-days. These three strategic actions become simultaneous initiatives.

↗ ↗ ↗

Addressing the Church's Current Situation

With a sense of urgency established and a covenant of agreement in place, the interim pastor is now ready to begin a thorough assessment of the church's current situation. Investigation would include interviews and conversations with current leaders and long-tenured members.

More than any church assessment instrument or tool is the interim pastor's intuition in hearing people tell the story of the church from their perspective. Careful attention should be given to their views and convictions of what happened in the exit of the previous pastor. In the case of long-tenured members, three questions can be helpful: What is your assessment of how the church is doing? What issues do you believe need to be addressed during the pastoral transition period? What is your hope for the future.

A Testimony from Ogea

These interviews and conversations may be scheduled or impromptu, one-to-one, or group interactions. In my consideration of one church, the travel distance involved a three-and-one half hour drive, necessitating a planned initial conversation. The approach was a weekend format involving a Saturday evening meal with key leaders, preaching on Sunday morning, followed by a lunch meeting with all the deacons. After lunch, I asked the deacons attending to sit with me in a large circle. I began the meeting with a brief statement of why I was there and my purpose in asking for this meeting. I then proposed a question to the group: How long have you been a member of this church? Everyone responded, many with their heart-felt convictions of the current state of the church. The average years of membership of the deacons present was 30 years! (This church had experienced a forty-year decline, involving four pastors – one resigned over a moral failure and another was force-terminated). I then made a statement and asked a second question: It's obvious that all of you have stayed here during the duration of decline. What do you think it would take for the church to revitalize? Again, all responded – many of them with heavy emotion. The meeting lasted two hours!

Along with interviews and conversations with current leaders and long-tenured members, a more structured approach to assessing the current situation would be to establish a transition focus team. This team could be like an ad-hoc committee, appointed for the purpose of preparing the church for the next pastor. This transition focus team would work sequentially with the PSC to eliminate duplicity in function. This team might also only meet for a short period of time and then share their findings and conclusions with the PSC, infusing their process.[1]

A Testimony from Echols

The process of choosing the transition focus team can vary. One way allows the congregation to nominate potential people to serve. From this list, an appropriate group can select the ones to serve. The number can be flexible. For smaller churches that have less than 75 in attendance, from seven to ten might work well. Larger churches would want a minimum of twenty to as many as forty. An attempt should be made to represent as much of a cross section of the congregation as possible.

A Testimony from Ogea

One church that engaged me as interim pastor already had a transition focus team in place, according to their bylaws. This team would be activated when a pastor vacancy occurred and was tasked with duties and responsibilities during the period of pastoral transition, one of which specifically involved working closely with an interim pastor.

1 A detailed discussion of the formation, responsibilities, and utilization of a transition focus team can be found in the Transitional Pastor Ministry Training Manual.

The transition focus team will attempt to answer the following:[2]

1. What is our mission? A mission statement defines why the church exists. This is the biblical mandate that every church should consider, encompassing the five great purposes of the church:

   - evangelism
   - discipleship
   - worship
   - ministry
   - fellowship

2. What is our heritage? The team should explore the following:

   - A reminder of the provision of God
   - A reminder of the providence of God
   - A reminder of the power of the word of God
   - A reminder of the immutable purposes of God
   - A reminder of the importance of the people of God

3. What are our distinctive characteristics that make us unique from other congregations in our proximity? The thoughts below could assist in defining no more than ten characteristics:

   - Every human being is fearfully and wonderfully made (Psalm 139:14) and is special and unique in God's sight as are the distinctiveness of every human fingerprint. Churches are the same.
   - Every church has a distinctive but critical role (For the body is not one member but many- I Cor. 12: 14). What is that role?
   - What can our church do that is unique but also complementary to all our sister churches in the city and area and for the Kingdom of God as a whole?

---

2 If the church in pastoral transition has never experienced this function of a transition focus team and establishing these parameters, then sufficient time must be taken to discuss, develop, and articulate these components with the transition focus team. Much of this development will be included in the pastor profile. If a transition focus team concept already exists, then sufficient time must be taken to review and revise these components once the transition focus team is activated.

4. What are our opportunities and challenges? Some relevant aspects to explore include the external demographics of the community in relation to how they match or differ from internal demographics of the church and the ten-year or twenty-year data history of the church. Both long-term and short-term trends are important to examine.

5. What is our vision? Vision is how the mission is enacted in the real-time setting of the congregation. A vision statement declares what the church envisions in a reasonable timeframe. It is seen and felt from the moment you walk onto the campus of the church or experience it outside the physical setting of the church in how the church carries on its ministry outside of the walls of its buildings.[3]

A Testimony from Ogea

To begin to establish a new vision for the future engages an important discussion. This new vision should be included in the pastor profile developed by the pastor search committee (See Part Three). One caution would be to resist too much detailed development of a future vision, allowing for the new pastor to influence this initiative in the first year or two of his tenure.

Essentially, the mission is the same for all churches. Words expressing the mission may vary, but the fundamental mission is the same in the biblical mandates. However, each church embraces how to engage the mission in a contextual vision statement, which can be subdivided into issues and/or actions to be addressed. The timeline of a pastoral transition offers a transforming opportunity for solving problems, resolving conflicts, and managing crises.

---

3 See William E. Hull, *Strategic Preaching: The Role of the Pulpit in Pastoral Leadership* (St. Louis: Chalice Press, 2006), pp. 116-120. Hull identified purpose, context, vision, and mission as the essential components crucial to the life of a church or Christian organization. He defined mission as what a church does "to fulfill its purpose in a particular context in such a way as to actualize its vision." Vision is set squarely in the future "as an incentive and aspiration that cannot be collapsed into the status quo."

↗ ↗ ↗

A Plan of Action for Solving Problems, Resolving Conflicts, and Managing Crises

As discussed in Part One, the critical function of the interim pastor to engage in conflict resolution and crisis management must be included in the covenant of agreement. This allows the interim pastor to begin immediately addressing existing problems, conflicts, and/or crises, which remain unsolved. In our first meetings with deacons, key committees, church staff, and a transition focus team, we ask the question: "What issues or problems exist here, that could be addressed or solved during these days of pastoral transition, and if resolved, would be a blessing to the next pastor?" Synthesizing the responses of this question enables the interim pastor to form a plan of action.[4]

Solving existing problems and resolving existing conflicts necessitates several questions:

1. What are the causes, or antecedents of the problem or conflict?
2. What are the indicators, or issues of the problem or conflict?
3. What is the intensity level of the problem or conflict?
4. What are solutions or alternatives to the problem or conflict?
5. What is the best or acceptable solution to the problem or conflict?

In *Every Congregation Needs a Little Conflict*, George Bullard defined congregational conflict as "a struggle of at least two persons or groups seeking to occupy the same space at the same time." He identified congregational conflict in three categories: healthy, transitional, or unhealthy. These categories can occur at the intrapersonal level, the interpersonal level, the inter-group or sub-system level, and at

4 In many situations, ongoing problems and conflicts exist as unresolved and may have been unresolved for an extended period of time. However, we can testify, in uncanny evidence, that conflicts can erupt during the pastoral transition journey that require and demand immediate attention. These conflicts do not classify as ongoing – they occur suddenly or quickly, often the unintended consequences of unhealthy or benign conflicts.

the organism, organization, or system-wide level.[5] In *When Church Conflict Happens*, Michael Hare discussed benign conflict in addition to unhealthy and healthy conflict. He defined benign conflict as disagreements that occur because of unintentional organizational deficits and oversights.[6]

Bullard identified seven Intensity Levels of Congregational Conflict.[7] He unpacks each intensity level in a full chapter of overview, illustrations, and coaching insights. The first three intensity levels define healthy congregational conflict. Intensity Level One involves identifiable, task-oriented problems with many solutions. Intensity Level Two identifies relationship-oriented disagreements over multiple issues. Intensity Level Three represents competition within a group or between groups. The first two conflict intensity levels represent problems and disagreements, which offer an opportunity for quick and immediate solutions, and which can be addressed by the interim pastor taking a chaplain or personal coach approach. The third conflict intensity level occurs when the first two intensity levels are handled improperly or incorrectly, resulting in escalation. In these situations, the interim pastor must take the mediator approach.

Bullard's three intensity levels of healthy conflict provide an excellent template for answering the first three questions. In addressing most existing problems and conflicts, the answers to the first three questions can be settled in one conversation or meeting. In most situations, the causes, or antecedents of the problem or conflict can be identified quickly. The typical indicators of declining attendance and scarce finances are the most obvious presenting issues, but they may not tell the full picture. Lack of vision, inward focus, depletion of volunteerism, poor communication, and

---

5 George W. Bullard, Jr., *Every Congregation Needs a Little Conflict* (St. Louis: Chalice Press, 2008),, p. 10. Bullard's textbook serves as an excellent handbook for conflict resolution. Of added value is his chapters on leadership styles for engaging conflict, processes for engaging conflict, how to never experience unhealthy conflict in you congregation again, and implications for denominational service alongside congregations.

6 Michael Hare, *When Church Conflict Happens: A Proven Process for Resolving Unhealthy Disagreements and Embracing Healthy Ones* (Chicago: Moody Press, 2019), p. 21.

7 See "The Intensity Levels of Congregational Conflict" chart in Bullard, *Every Congregation Needs a Little Conflict*, p. 17

passive aggressive behavior are all signs of conflict.

However, other existing problems and conflicts may require more investigation and may require the interim pastor to do "some homework" – researching previous business/congregational meeting minutes, examining church bylaws, evaluating historical church profile data, or auditing policies and procedures.

If the established intensity level of an existing problem or conflict is identified as a Level One, Two, or Three, then proceed to questions four and five previously listed. If, however, the existing problem or conflict intensity level has moved beyond Level Three, then a different approach must be taken regarding solutions and alternatives. (See A Caution from Ogea below)

A Testimony from Echols

One church had a rift between the congregation and the deacons that led a significant number of the congregation to believe that the previous pastor had left out of frustration in working with the deacons. That was partly true, but it was much more complicated. The previous pastor had attempted to use an authoritative style of leadership over the deacons when they had been used to a collaborative style. After spending considerable time with the deacons and those who blamed the deacons, I discovered that significant misunderstanding and miscommunication perpetrated the division. As a result of the church being in steep decline, both sides were seeking to find a scapegoat to blame. In this instance, focusing on the envisioning process was a means of mitigating the disunity in the congregation. It is of utmost importance for the interim pastor to emphasize that the Holy Spirit is at work to bring the congregation together in a common biblical vision for the future.

A Caution from Ogea

Intensity Level Four pinpoints transitional intensity between healthy conflict and unhealthy conflict. While every congregation needs healthy conflict, no congregation needs escalation to level four, where competition within a group or between groups shifts to church-wide competition with voting. If resolution does not occur at this transitional level, then the conflict escalates to levels five, six, or seven, resulting in congregational damage often irreparable.

According to Bullard, unhealthy conflict levels require "conflict literacy, emotional maturity, and spiritual maturity not seen in the typical congregation. They also require outside, third-party assistance to address them."[8] We mentioned earlier that most interim pastors can function as "seasoned veterans" in conflict resolution and crisis management because of their previous congregational leadership experience. That is true. Because of my lengthy pastoral and denominational experience in dealing with churches and ministry organizations experiencing high levels of intensity, I (Ogea) can function in most situations as the "third-party assistance" that Bullard refers to. However, the interim pastor who does not have specialized experience in conflict mediation or arbitration should not be hesitant to seek another expert as third-party assistance.

Though similar to situations of conflict, crises group into two categories: (1) unplanned, accidental, or unforeseeable catastrophes – a weather-related event resulting in cataclysmic destruction, such as a hurricane, tornado, wildfire, or flood; a violent act or vicious malevolence; or an accidental tragedy. (2) personal and congregational situations which erupt into destructive circumstances – the disintegration of a minister's family, brooding dissension and disagreement in the church family which suddenly escalates into a high-intensity level of conflict, or a combination of the two. The convergence of conflict resolution and crises management produces a challenging and intentional leadership process during pastoral transitions.[9]

8 Bullard, p. 14.

9 See Steve Echols and Allen England, *Catastrophic Crisis: Ministry Leadership in the Midst of Trial and Tragedy*, Nashville: B & H Academic, 2011 and H. Dan O'Hair and Mary John O'Hair, *Communication and Catastrophic Events: Strategic Risk and Crisis Management*, Hoboken, NJ: John Wiley and Sons, Inc., 2023.

A Testimony from Ogea

I became the interim pastor of a church one-year into the COVID-19 pandemic. The church was struggling to return to pre-COVID worship attendance because of the rigid restrictions of public gatherings and congregational fear of contracting the virus. While some of the small group Sunday School classes had resumed, attendance lagged behind pre-COVID levels as well. Then, just three months into my tenure as interim pastor, a devastating hurricane roared through south Louisiana, causing massive damage to the church's worship center, rendering it uninhabitable. Fortunately, the fellowship hall had once been the worship space, so with minimal renovation, we could convert it back to a worship venue and resume worship after several weeks of disruption. The double "wammy" of a widespread pandemic plus the unforeseeable catastrophic disaster of a hurricane proved a huge challenge.

We agree with Bullard: "If you believe there is hope for the next world, if you believe that death is not the ultimate, if you believe that out of failure can come new life, new opportunity, new growth and hope, then conflict can be a positive motivating force."[10]

↗ ↗ ↗

Establishing the Priority of Preaching and the Enhancement of Worship

As we previously discussed in Part One, the covenant of agreement clarifies our three key functions as the interim pastor. The first function defines the priority of preaching and the enhancement of worship: Serve as the preacher and worship leader for the Sunday

10 Bullard, p. 14

AM and/or PM services, and Wednesday evenings when possible or available. When the distance prohibits both Sundays and Wednesdays, then the Sunday preaching and worship planning engagement become primary. Even though we confirm emphatically that we are not interested in just being the interim preacher, preaching and worship leadership provide the most effective function of our relationship with the church during the period of pastoral transition.

Since our context in this handbook relates directly to churches in need of revitalization, the immediate focus of preaching and worship planning must speak immediately and directly to encouragement, hope, optimism, and vision. Regardless of the prevailing circumstances, churches experience a myriad of emotions during a pastoral transition.

1. Some in the congregation who were close to the pastor and his family experience a sense of loss while others express a sense of relief.

2. Some are unsettled about the future and others are excited about potential changes for the future.

3. Some understand the need for patience in the search for the next pastor while others wish to move quickly to fill the pastoral vacancy.

The greatest need in a church moving into a pastoral transition is to address immediately the preaching and proclamation issue. In our experience, churches who wait too long to determine who will be the consistent "voice in the pulpit" or who decide to line up a series of "guest preachers" create a sense of unsettled anxiety. And if that sense of unsettled anxiety becomes the "the new norm," weekly worship attendance and giving potential will decline. To say it another way, congregants in churches where the primacy of preaching is the highest expectation of weekly worship can lose their focus and commitment quickly.

A Testimony from Ogea

Two churches in my interim pastor experience waited eight months from the departure of their pastor to the decision to engage me as the interim pastor. In the first month, each week at the end of a worship service, the members were coming to me consistently with statements like: "Thanks for coming to help us." "We've missed hearing a consistent preaching voice every Sunday." "We heard some great sermons each week from our guest preachers, but there was no consistency or continuity." The quickest way to establish encouragement, hope, optimism and vision is through the priority of preaching and the enhancement of worship.

We believe that churches in need of revitalization in a pastoral transition situation need to be reminded often to "stand with your back to the past facing the future" and "the best is yet to be." The priority of preaching in the first 60-days should focus on sermons that reinforce the purposes of the church and the present future of the church. Reggie McNeal coined the term "present future" early in the 21st century – we believe that his assessment and conviction still ring true:

> The present makes clearest sense in light of the future. We humans write history by looking at the past. God creates history ahead of time. He never forecasts. God always backcasts. He began with the end in mind. The future is always incipient in the present. Before the foundation of the world, the Lamb was slain. Calvary was anticipated in God's kiss of life into Adam. The cross gains dimension silhouetted against the empty tomb. The empty tomb confirmed the invasion of the future into the present. When Paul encountered the resurrected Jesus, he realized the future had been fast-forwarded. That changed everything. It still does.[11]

---

11 Reggie McNeal, *The Present Future: Six Tough Questions for the Church* (San Francisco: Jossey-Bass, 2003), p. xi.

Because a timeline of how long a pastoral transition will last cannot be predicted, providing pastoral leadership through preaching presents the interim pastor with rich options:

1. Individual, "stand-alone" sermons, for example, from biblical texts that remind the church of a God who empowers, delivers, enables, heals, provides, and shepherds His people; and a Risen Christ who comforts, encourages, equips, and protects His church.

2. Series of sermons which take a thematic approach from Bible books: Exodus, Joshua, Nehemiah, the Psalms, the Gospels (especially the resurrection narratives), the Acts of the Apostles, I Corinthians, and Revelation.

3. Special days sermons, particularly around Christmas, New Years and Easter.

The interim pastor must be sensitive to the needs of the congregation in his preaching. J. Daniel Bauman noted four purposes of preaching: kerygmatic, didactic, therapeutic, and social prophetic.[12] All of these are important in pastoral transition. Kerygmatic, or evangelistic is always a priority and seeing souls come to Christ matters for all eternity and greatly encourages the church. Didactic, or doctrinal can develop believers and address any theological weaknesses or errors in the church. Therapeutic preaching provides biblical comfort for hurting people. Social -prophetic is always relevant in bringing the truth of God's Word to the issues of the day.

A Testimony from Ogea and Echols

In our experience, we conclude that therapeutic preaching is important, because individuals and the church often need healing, regardless of the circumstances triggering the pastoral transition.

12 J. Daniel Bauman, *Introduction to Contemporary Preaching* (Grand Rapids: Baker Book House, 1972) pp. 207-219.

We believe that a fifth purpose should be added to Bauman's four – strategic preaching. This category presents a vision of what it means to be the people of God in the context in which they minister. Strategic preaching lays the biblical groundwork for discovering the mission and vision of the church. All of these aspects will be covered when the Scripture is preached in a faithful expository manner. However, being sensitive to the status of the church can lead the interim pastor to emphasize a certain type. For instance, the congregation may especially need a fresh perspective for their vision through strategic preaching. If significant conflict has occurred or the church has experienced tragedy or other unsettling circumstances, then therapeutic preaching may need to be emphasized. The effective interim pastor will sense and follow the leading of the Holy Spirit.

Because we believe that the interim pastor functions as both preacher and worship leader, we seek to model these two functions in the journey of pastoral transition. Nothing engages, empowers, and encourages the congregation more than celebratory worship experiences. We often say that our overall task as the interim pastor is to "work our way out of a job" and get the church ready for their next pastor. We are serious about presenting the next pastor with an excited and expectant church. The priority of preaching and the enhancement of worship take center stage in creating excitement and expectancy.

↗

PART THREE

The Pastor Search Committee: Administering the Process of Searching for a New Pastor

CHURCHES SELECT AND ELECT a PSC for the special and spiritual assignment of searching for and selecting the next pastor.[1] The task may seem daunting, and requires immense time, energy, and commitment. In God's omniscience, He already knows the "who" and "when." God knows just what each church needs. God knows where the next pastor resides. The Pastor Search Committee must seek God's will and trust God's

1 Individual churches select and elect pastor search committees in processes aligned with either their defined policies or past procedures. Some churches define their PSC selection and election in their church bylaws. Others select and elect based on their immediate past pastoral vacancy. The authors' experiences agree that churches select and elect persons who represent their current congregational constituencies, who are respected by virtue of their trust within the congregation, and who will maintain integrity in their search process. This team will determine and present to the congregation the final candidate and ask for their affirmation. The question of "how many should serve on the PSC" usually mirrors the size of the church, but in most cases, a minimum of five and maximum of nine serves as an average number. The choice of an odd number allows for any "tie votes" that may occur in decision-making. Some churches select and elect the PSC members and two alternates, in case one or more of the members elected is unable to serve for the duration of the search.

foreknowledge. When God's will and the pastor search connect, then God's man is placed in God's church.

The duties and details of the Pastor Search Committee can be summarized in four broad components: "Before the Search," "The Search," "Steps to the Call," and "Setting the New Pastor in Place." (We will cover the first two in Part Three and the last two in Part Four)

↗ ↗ ↗

Before the Search

1. PRAY – PRAY – PRAY. The single-most important task of the PSC involves consistent and constant prayer. Praying together forms a spiritual bond and a tight cohesiveness. Synergy and teamwork allow the PSC to function at the highest level of excellence. We urge the PSC to pray consistently and constantly for unity, vision, and wisdom.

- Pray for **unity** within the committee. The PSC must pledge among themselves to guard confidentiality at all times and at all costs. Any violation of confidentiality erodes trust, weakens respect and creates dysfunction. While well-meaning fellow church members, family, and colleagues will probe for "inside information," PSC members must resist all pressure to share information about potential candidates. We agree with Tom Harris and George Bullard: "You owe it to each candidate and your church to maintain confidentiality. One leak on social media can start a wildfire of rumors and speculation that can damage the candidate's relationship with his current church."[2]

- Pray for the future **vision** of the church and the next pastor. The PSC must be the "forward thinkers" during the pastoral transition. Regardless of the circumstances, reasons, or situations resulting in

2 Tom Harris and George Bullard, *Soaring Between Pastors: 8 Actions to Thrive During a Pastoral Transition* (Wheaton, IL: Big Snowy Media, 2021), 165. See also John W. Utley, *Navigating Pastoral Transitions* (Fort Worth: Cotton House Press, 2024), pp. 44-46, for "Confidentiality and Ethical Guidelines for Pastor Search Committees."

the pastoral vacancy, the future vision of the church should capture the full attention of the PSC before the actual pastor search begins. One common mistake and misstep occurs when PSCs consider candidates before the future vision for the church is established. We counsel PSCs to not begin the examination of candidate resumes and profiles this early in the process. Resumes and recommendations of potential candidates may arrive as soon as the pastoral vacancy becomes public knowledge. However, the PSC should resist the temptation to begin their examination of potential candidates prior to completing this "Before the Search" initiative.

- Pray for **wisdom** during the search. Serving on a PSC defines both a privileged honor and a complex commitment. In a Baptist context, governed congregationally, a PSC is considered an ad hoc committee by selection instead of appointment. Baptist churches select trusted leaders who represent the constituent make-up of the congregation. A PSC may include people who have served on previous searches or may involve people who have never served. While considered an honor to be selected, the PSC soon discovers that the search process will involve a complex commitment of time, energy, and persistence. The addition of regular meetings, often weekly, requires committee members to adjust work, church, and family responsibilities. Certain stages of the search demand individual or group functions in between the weekly meetings. These considerations necessitate constant prayer for wisdom, both collective wisdom and individual wisdom.[3]

A Testimony from Echols

I recommend that the church appoint a team to lead the church in praying for the pastor search process. During the time the church is in the search process, it would be spiritually uplifting to have two or three special Sunday night services

3 One way to keep the PSC and the church family connected in prayer is to establish a Scriptural theme. One church developed a "Pray Ezra 7:10" theme, challenging the church family to pray for the pastor search process every day at 7:10 AM and 7:10 PM, utilizing Ezra 7:10 – "Now Ezra had determined in his heart to study the law of the Lord, obey it, and teach its statutes and ordinances in Israel." (CSB – Christian Standard Bible)

where the main emphasis is prayer. Though most churches no longer have Sunday night services, I found these services have been well-attended.[4]

2. Conduct a Congregational Survey. A key consideration regarding the development of the Pastor Profile involves the capture of the congregation's convictions and mindset. A congregational survey offers a useful instrument to determine the congregation's mindset and conviction regarding the next pastor.[5] Many helpful examples of congregational surveys exist. We suggest that the PSC examine several congregational survey samples, personalizing the survey they deem essential for their congregational context. The personalized and contextualized survey should involve both general questions and specific questions. Once the PSC agrees on the survey's content, the congregational survey is then distributed.[6]

Special Note

Two cautions warrant consideration. One, the PSC must ensure confidentiality in receiving the individual surveys. We suggest that the surveys remain anonymous without requiring signatures on the survey. We suggest also that the individual members of the PSC should be the only ones who receive the surveys from congregants. We suggest further that both hard copies and electronic copies be available to congregants. A three-to-four-week window for returning the surveys should be sufficient for maximum participation.

4 See Appendix D: Sample Prayer Services, developed by the Ministerial Staff of First Baptist Church, Lyons, GA and First Baptist Church, Vidalia, GA.

5 One church decided to circulate a Church Leader Survey in place of a Congregational Survey. (See Appendix E)

6 See Appendix F. The Georgia Baptist Convention's online Pastor Search Committee training includes downloadable charts, rubrics, surveys and assessments, all in PDF format: https://gabaptist.org/resources/pastor-search-committee-training)

3. PSC completes a church health assessment. The PSC would benefit from completing a church health assessment to measure and monitor current reality. This action could be done simultaneously to conducting the congregational survey. Pastor search committees owe it to themselves and the future pastor to accept current reality instead of alternate reality. Medical professionals routinely engage their patients in a health assessment – a set of questions, answered by patients, that asks about personal behaviors, risks, life-changing events, health goals and priorities, and overall health. Diagnosis and treatment occur after the completion of a health assessment, not before.

Several church health assessment tools exist. I (Ogea) utilize most often the church health assessment developed by Gene Getz, entitled "33 Questions to Evaluate Your Church's Health." I prefer to provide the PSC members with a hard copy of the assessment, with instructions for each person to complete the assessment individually. The PSC should develop a group consensus for all 33 questions.[7]

4. Compose an Executive Summary of the congregational survey and the church health assessment. The church health assessment summary and the congregational survey results can now form the template to develop a prospective pastor profile. This executive summary should be shared with the interim/transitional pastor for input and insight. Some PSCs may consider sharing the executive summary with other church leaders, or in the case of medium-sized and larger churches, the church staff. Sharing the executive summary with key church leaders and/or church staff creates a "feedback loop."

---

7 Gene Getz, https://bibletolife.com/resources/articles/33-questions-to-evaluate-your-churchs-health, Published on October 7, 2021. Modified on September 9, 2022. **Leadership Transformations, Inc.** offers an online Church Health Assessment Tool (CHAT), which can be accessed at https://healthychurch.net/church-health-assessment-tool.htm. **Assist Church Expansion** utilizes a Church Health Check-up, which can be downloaded at https://assistcx.org/wp-content/uploads/2018/09/Church-Health-Assessment-Form.pdf. **Church Answers** promotes a Church Health Scorecard, which can be downloaded at https://churchanswers.com/solutions/tools/church-health-scorecard/church-health-scorecard.

Special Note

The church health assessment and congregational survey executive summary should NOT be distributed for public view and feedback. If the public domain of the congregation gets involved at this point, internal discussions will create opinions and preferences which could sidetrack and sabotage the search process.

5. Develop a prospective Pastor Profile.[8] Taking the time to develop a pastor profile results in a tremendous time-saver when the PSC begins to consider resumes of viable candidates. A pastor profile should address the personality identity and leadership identity of prospective pastoral candidates, with the goal of alignment between the pastoral candidate identity and the congregational identity.

A pastor profile defines the personality identity of the next pastor. This answers the "who" question. The personality identity describes the age range, family situation, ministerial experience, educational component, etc. of viable candidates. These components should assist the PSC in determining candidates that would be the right fit as the next pastor. Although the PSC should be specific in defining each of the personality identity components, flexibility also should be maintained. Very seldom will a candidate exhibit ALL of the personality identity components. The PSC will need to consider which of the personality identity components are "deal breakers" and which one or ones can be flexed.

---

8 Excellent and helpful examples of building pastor profiles exist in PSC handbooks and training manuals. Many SBC State Conventions list these handbooks and training manuals on their websites as downloadable documents. In addition to these downloadable examples, three other PSC handbooks offer pastor profile examples as well: *The Pastor Search Committee Handbook*, by Lifeway.com; *Search*, by William Vanderbloemen; *How to Find the Right Pastor*, by Ron Hunter Jr. and David C Gibbs, III. PSC committees should examine several examples and personalize/customize their pastor profiles. See Appendix G: Senior Pastor Search Notice and Pastor Profile Example.

A Testimony from Dr. Ogea

A situation in a recent church interim involved a pastor profile which defined significant senior pastor experience as one of the personality identity components. When the PSC narrowed their search to their final two candidates, both of the candidates matched strongly the personality components in all areas except one: neither of them had senior pastor experience. However, because both candidates matched every other personality component, the PSC decided to move forward to the interview stage. One of these candidates connected with the PSC in such a powerful way that the lack of senior pastor experience did not serve as a "deal breaker," and the PSC unanimously settled on this candidate as their recommended choice.

A pastor profile describes also the leadership identity of the next pastor. This answers the "what" question. The leadership identity chronicles theological positions, doctrinal beliefs, pastoral leadership methodologies, length of tenure in current and past positions, etc. of viable candidates. Generally, the resumes of viable candidates will indicate these leadership identity components. However, the PSC may need to investigate beyond the resume to verify the leadership identity components. This is where reference checks, described later in this section, must be questioned thoroughly, with detailed regard to leadership identity. Always remember that past behavior is the best predictor of future behavior.

Special Note

An interim/transitional pastor can be open, honest, and strategic in leading the PSC toward their next pastor only if he is NOT a candidate for the permanent pastor. The interim pastor's only agenda and function is to provide effective leadership in the transition and to focus on the church's future revitalization. Leading the PSC to develop a pastor profile early in the search process hinges on the interim pastor being totally objective and removed as a potential candidate. In our experience, PSC members and church members will express their desire for the interim pastor to consider the permanent pastoral role, but the interim pastor must resist all temptations and overtures. It is the conviction of both of us (Echols and Ogea) that the interim/transitional pastor should not be a viable candidate to become the next permanent pastor of the congregation. Certainly, successful exceptions exist with interim/transitional pastors becoming either the bi-vocational, (or co-vocational) pastor, or transitioning to become the full-time pastor.

↗ ↗ ↗

The Search

With the completion of the "Before the Search" initiatives, the PSC is now ready to focus on "The Search" stage of collecting and vetting resumes of viable candidates. During the "Before the Search" phase, resumes and recommendations of potential candidates may arrive from several venues.

- Candidates who "apply" for the position, submitting their own resumes for consideration.
- Church members who share the name or resume of a candidate.
- Recommendations from the public domain who hear of the pastoral vacancy.

Special Note

We urge the PSC, with strong caution, to avoid the temptation of considering these early candidate submissions until the official search is launched.

1. Collect resumes of prospective pastors.[9] Several options exist regarding sources of prospective pastor candidate resumes. Most national and regional denominational organizations will collect resumes of candidates searching for positions and distribute these resumes to their constituent churches by request. Southern Baptists (SBC) organize themselves by state conventions and associations within those conventions. In addition to state conventions and associations, the SBC conducts its work through eleven ministry entities, including the International Mission Board (IMB), the North American Mission Board (NAMB), and six theological seminaries. Many of these organizations provide platforms for churches to post their pastoral vacancies.

Special Note

A word of caution regarding receiving resumes from the aforementioned entities. This results often in the committee being flooded. The results of such a method are mixed. Sometimes the committees can struggle to have viable candidates. This method can greatly assist in getting resumes. However, many of the gathered resumes will have red flags or do not fit the profile the committee has developed. Also, resumes may still be activated on the entity's job boards which should have been deactivated when the candidate accepted a new church position.

A Testimony from Echols

In one church, the PSC tried on two different occasions to utilize the job board of the state convention. Both times the

9 For example, the Louisiana Baptist Convention website (www.louisianabaptists.org) offers a resume service which allows pastors to search for positions and churches to post positions. The offices and leaders of associations of the state conventions may collect resumes of prospective pastors that can be shared with pastor search committees by request. The New Orleans Baptist Theological Seminary Church Ministry Relations office (www.nobts.edu/cmr) provides a platform for students/alumni to view open jobs and post their resumes that can be sent to prospective employers (churches) upon request.

> pastor search team got bogged down with the large number of resumes. They never were able to come up with a strong candidate from the more than one hundred resumes they received.

Here is a suggested strategy for pastor search committees to gather potential pastoral candidates:

- Prepare a cover letter on the church's stationery, signed by the PSC chairperson and the interim pastor. State in the cover letter what you are requesting, give a timeline (3-4 weeks), indicating the address of where the resumes are to be received. If the church address and/or a member of the PSC is utilized to receive resumes, great safeguards must be placed so that only one person receives the resumes and retains them on behalf of the PSC.

- Gather names and addresses of state convention executive directors, associational mission strategists, seminary presidents/faculty, selected pastors, etc. We (Ogea and Echols) believe that this list should be selective and personally addressed to those leaders who would consider the request for potential candidates seriously and who would be prompt in response.

- Mail the cover letter, with the pastor profile included, to the selected leaders. Once the deadline stated in the cover letter arrives, follow-up contacts with those who have not responded are appropriate.

2. Narrow the search to the top five (or less).[10] Once resumes are received, depending on the number of resumes received, the PSC may choose to divide into small groups to cull the resumes, with each small group reporting to the whole. To narrow to the top five candidates may require several rounds of collaborative discussion.[11]

---

10 See Ron Hunter Jr. and David C. Gibbs III, *How to Find the Right Pastor,* (Nashville: Randall House, 2023), pp. 120-153. The authors provide strong, step-by-step guidance on finding and narrowing to your top 3 to 5 candidates.

11 See Appendix H for a sample Candidate Ranking chart.

Special Note

Do not proceed until agreement is reached by the PSC regarding the top candidates.

A Testimony from Ogea

In one church, internal disagreement occurred between the PSC chairman and vice-chairman, unknown to me. When the PSC narrowed the search to a top two, these two leaders clashed "behind the scenes". When a vote of the committee occurred to select the top candidate, the vote was not unanimous. I counseled the PSC to pause and pray, but consensus could not be reached. The vice-chairman agreed to relent for the sake of unity. Although the PSC then moved to Candidate #2, (who became the next pastor), tension and hesitancy brooded within the PSC during the "call to the church" process. In hindsight, I should have paused and worked from within the PSC to regain unity and consensus.

3. Listen to sermons of the top candidates. Although preaching defines only one component of the leadership identity of pastoral candidates, it is essential for the PSC to listen to multiple sermons of the selected candidates. The PSC may gather as a group to listen to sermons in one setting, or the top five candidates can each be assigned to one member of the PSC for viewing. For most potential candidates, sermons can be viewed on their church websites. In cases where no sermons exist in the public domain, the PSC can request that the potential candidates forward sermons for examination.[12]

4. Contact the top candidates and get their permission to do a background check.[13] The PSC could do their own

12 The Candidate Ranking chart lists a category for evaluation of sermons (Preaching rank).

13 Background checks should include credit, criminal, education verification, and employment record verification, including ministry positions verification.

background checks, which can be a time-consuming process. For a fee, companies and agencies exist which can do these background checks. Denominational agencies and organizations often contract with companies or agencies who will engage in these background checks on behalf of their constituency churches.

5. Develop a questionnaire to send to the top candidates. The prospective pastor questionnaire should involve both general and specific questions related to theological and doctrinal issues, ministry practice, and leadership convictions. The questionnaire can be divided into questions of common agreement, individual questions and yes/no questions.[14]

The prospective pastor questionnaire should be shared with the top candidates simultaneously, with an established deadline for return. From experience, the questionnaire may become a "deal breaker" when received by the candidates. When candidates receive the questionnaire, they must determine if they wish to remain in consideration for the vacant pastoral opportunity. Potential candidates who do not wish to be considered further, in most cases, will not complete the questionnaire. The PSC can review all completed questionnaires and evaluate responses "question-by-question."

6. Rank the candidates in "order of priority" to proceed. After evaluating sermons, conducting background checks, and comparing questionnaires, the PSC is ready to rank the candidates in order of priority. We recommend that the PSC proceed from this point forward with only one candidate at a time. Proceeding with more than one candidate at a time becomes a challenging undertaking and can result in confusion and disagreement within the PSC.

A Testimony from Ogea

Only by rare exception did I recommend the PSC consider two candidates simultaneously. While serving a recent church, the PSC followed the process outlined in this chapter.

14 See Appendix I for a sample Prospective Pastor Questionnaire.

The PSC narrowed to a top three. One of the candidates removed himself from consideration by not completing the Questionnaire. Another candidate proceeded through all eight "steps," but withdrew to consider another church. The third candidate proceeded through all eight steps, including a preliminary interview, but eventually removed himself from consideration, responding that he could not "receive peace from the Lord to leave his current church." In the meantime, two other potential candidates surfaced, who were not in the original mix of consideration. When the PSC reviewed credentials, they determined that these two new candidates fit the pastor profile. Due to the extended timeline and the possibility of expediting the process, they felt confident to consider both new candidates simultaneously.

7. **Check all references on the top candidate's resume.** Most resumes will list several references with contact information. Assigning a reference to each member of the PSC to contact prescribes the most effective method. We suggest emailing the reference to set up a phone interview. Of extreme importance, with little variation, the references should be asked the same questions for information continuity. Reference checks can be completed often within a week's time, allowing for the PSC to compare notes and debrief at their next meeting. If nothing shared by the references causes pause or concern, then the PSC proceeds to the next step.

Special Note

We recommend going beyond the references listed on a resume and checking references not listed. Every candidate is very likely to have friends that will speak highly of him. The committee needs to hear non-biased assessments from pastors and others in the community where he currently serves. Two ways of locating the identify of "other references": (1) Contacting the local Associational Missions Strategist can lead to discovering those who can give a reference. (2) When contacting a candidate's references listed on the resume, the last question asked could be, "Would you recommend someone that we should contact about this candidate?" (3) In some cases, it may be good to consider hiring an investigating service although the cost of such services may be prohibitive to all but the very largest and best resourced congregations.

8. Contact the candidate and let him know that you are ready to proceed with him and only him at this time. Ask him to prayerfully consider if he is open to proceeding. If he is open to proceed, mail or email him a packet of information about the church, including the pastor profile, church bylaws, attendance and financial information, church organizational structure, 10-year church profile, etc.

Special Note

At any point in this "narrowing of the search," a pause or decision not to move forward could occur within the PSC or from the candidate himself. The PSC should be ready to respond, if this occurs, by moving ahead to the candidate "next in line." For this reason, ranking the top candidates becomes an essential step in the search process.

↗

PART FOUR

Calling and Welcoming a New Pastor

↗ ↗ ↗

Steps to the Call

The Search now completed and with full attention on the top candidate, the process now moves to "The Call" component. Four steps encompass The Call.

1. Preliminary interview with the candidate and the PSC. By this time, after several conversations between the Candidate and the PSC chairperson, a Preliminary Interview can be scheduled with the entire PSC. This interview can be done in-person or virtually. If in-person is doable, we suggest that a neutral location be chosen, perhaps meeting halfway if distance permits. If in-person is not doable, then a virtual interview works fine in most cases, utilizing the technology of Zoom, Google Meet, Microsoft Teams, etc.

Special Note

The PSC should agree on a list of questions to ask the candidate. These questions would be "in addition to" the questionnaire responses and/or "clarification" of the questionnaire responses of the Candidate. Reciprocally, the PSC should answer all of the Candidate's questions. Make sure that all "expectations" are dealt with – the PSC/Church's expectations and the Candidate's expectations.

Following this Preliminary Interview, the PSC should take adequate time to "debrief." After the debriefing, if no reason exists for pause, and if the PSC and the Candidate are in agreement, a Sunday could be scheduled to travel and hear the candidate preach in his church setting.[1]

Special Note

Depending on distance, the PSC may combine the Preliminary Interview of the Candidate and the Visit to the Candidate's church into one timeline. For example, the Interview could take place on Saturday afternoon/evening at the Candidate's location, with the PSC attending worship on Sunday morning.

2. Formal Interview with the Pastoral Candidate and Spouse. This formal interview should take place in the city, town, or community where the church is located, with the PSC serving as host. Great care and confidentiality must be involved in the location and time of this interview/meeting. The interview/meeting could occur at a location where a meal can be served. This interview/meeting should include a tour of the church facilities and a drive-through of the community. If scheduled after the church office hours, the Formal Interview could be held in the church facilities, with food catered-in, or at another location following the facilities tour. Major considerations for this formal interview include:

- The formal interview will build off of any previous discussions/conversations, and should include the Candidate's spouse. The

1 In today's world of video and audio capability, the PSC may determine that viewing recorded sermons and worship services would suffice in place of a visit to the Candidate's current church setting..

PSC needs to meet her, hear her heart/concerns, and experience the ethos of the ministry couple as a team.

- The formal interview will expand from the pastoral candidate questionnaire and previous discussions into more detailed and/or additional questions concerning theological issues, doctrinal convictions, leadership style, organizational structures, etc.

- The formal interview should address also all matters of compensation (salary, housing allowance, mileage reimbursement, insurance [health, life, etc.], retirement benefits, pastor's discretionary funds, civic club dues, conference and convention expenses, etc.)

- Presuming a movement toward an "In view of a call" invitation, the formal interview may disclose the church's obligations re: moving expenses, living arrangements and "transitions to the church field" issues and a start date in the new place of service.

- The formal interview should involve discussions about any and all expectations, including staff supervision, leadership with church committees and ministry teams, worship planning involvement, strategic planning engagement, outreach initiatives, etc.

- The goal of the formal interview – "every question asked and answered and all concerns and/or needs addressed." Hunter and Gibbs share wise counsel to the PSC concerning the goal of the formal interview:

  While you may feel knowledgeable about the candidate, the candidate still has much to process...When people anticipate a move, their primary concerns deal with what their lives will look like and how their daily needs will work. Where will they grocery shop? What are the school options? What is the cost of living? Will their spouse find employment if desired? Will their kids make friends? If a family member has special needs, will they be able to find medical specialists in the area?[2]

2 Hunter and Gibbs, *How to Find the Right Pastor*, p. 185.

Special Note

The Formal Interview/Meeting will take several hours. The PSC Committee should make arrangements for all meals, hotel expenses (if candidate and spouse are traveling from a distance), and mileage reimbursement.

3. "Reveal" Sunday. With all of the interviews, meetings, and considerations concluded, and both the PSC and the Pastoral Candidate in agreement, a Reveal Sunday can be executed. The Reveal Sunday occurs the Sunday before the Pastoral Candidate preaches "in view of a call." The Reveal Sunday identifies the Pastoral Candidate and his family to the congregation. The Reveal Sunday also announces the details of the "In View of a Call" weekend, including a special-called church congregational meeting to vote on the new pastor via a secret ballot.

Prepare a professionally-printed, information piece, to include a picture of the candidate and family (this picture can be used to display on the screen during the Reveal Sunday), biographical information, a written vision statement from the Pastoral Candidate, written testimonies from each of the PSC members, and a printed schedule of events for the "In View of a Call" weekend. This printed brochure is for distribution to the congregation at the time of the announcement. The PSC should serve as ushers of distribution, since they are the only ones who know the identity of the Candidate.

A Testimony from Ogea

As Interim Pastor, I allowed the PSC to individually share testimonies, which would consume most, if not all, of the preaching time in the worship service. I felt that the congregation should hear the hearts and convictions of each member of the PSC. I coached the PSC for each one to write a 2-3 minute testimony, assigning among themselves the topics to be discussed so as to eliminate repetition. Topics to be shared in the testimonies include: introduction of the pastor's family, a brief summary of the interviews, how this candidate matches the pastor profile, the qualifications of the candidate, why this candidate is a "good fit" for the church, and a brief reminder about the "In View of a Call Weekend events, etc. Since the church is already praying, it is certainly appropriate to end the worship service with the members of the PSC huddled together while inviting the congregation to move forward and surround them in prayer.

Special Note

Prior to the "Reveal Sunday", arrange for the pastoral candidate and the ministerial staff to meet together, to get acquainted, to discuss pastor/staff relations, and to talk strategy. This meeting may be scheduled in conjunction with the "In View of a Call" weekend events, or in-person between the Pastoral Candidate and the church staff if reasonable proximity exists, or by a virtual meeting.

4. "In View Of A Call" Weekend. After all of the above steps have been completed, and all involved are convinced of God's will to move forward, invite the Pastoral Candidate and his family to the church in view of a call as pastor. In most cases, this would encompass an entire weekend. Plan the weekend in a way that the congregation has ample time to meet him and his family and ask any questions they want to ask. A sample "in view of a call" weekend may include:

- A Friday evening meal with the Pastoral Candidate and spouse, church staff and spouses, deacons and spouses. (This could be expanded, according to the context, to include key leaders, committee chairpersons and ministry team leaders, and their spouses.) This important event will allow the key leaders of the church to meet the pastoral candidate and spouse, give opportunity for the candidate to speak to the group, and provide a time for Q & A.

- A Saturday afternoon/early evening dessert fellowship, inviting any and all church members who want to come meet the pastoral candidate and family. This "meet and greet" gathering could involve an opportunity for Q & A.

- Hear the pastoral candidate preach on Sunday morning, and vote by secret ballot at the conclusion of the worship service. The secret ballot is a simple "Yes" or "No" choice. The ballot should list the details of the call, including compensation, vacation and paid time-off, start date, etc. During the secret ballot vote, a member of the PSC can escort the Pastoral Candidate and family to an adjoining room to await the outcome. Once the votes are counted, the pastoral candidate and family are escorted back into the service, and the vote announced.

Special Note

The most common question: What is the percentage of "Yes" votes required by the Church and the Candidate for an official call? In some cases, the church by-laws will indicate the percentage needed to execute the call. If not previously determined, the decision should be made prior to the invitation for the "In View of a Call" weekend. The Candidate himself should be asked his minimum percentage of the ballot vote. Our strong suggestion mandates that the process should never get to point of a vote if any kind of pause or hesitation exists, even if it occurs during the "In View of a Call Weekend." Having a less than acceptable voting percentage would be cause for a loss of confidence between the PSC and the Church family. In our cumulative experience, we have never known of one situation that resulted in an unacceptable vote when the process proceeded positively and convincingly.

↗ ↗ ↗

Getting the New Pastor in Place

After a long, successful search process and the culmination of an exciting call of a new pastor, the focus now proceeds to getting the new pastor in place. The number of weeks between the 'vote to call" and the arrival of the new pastor and his family will vary. Our agreement as Interim Pastors includes staying through the transition period until the new pastor and his family arrive on the field.

The PSC must fulfill the responsibility of arranging moving expenses, transition details, and living arrangements of the new pastor and family. When the new pastor is transitioning from another church, he must resign his position and fulfill the time requirements of leaving that church. Every situation is different – the time between resignation and arrival can be a short two or three weeks, or may involve a much longer transition time. As soon as possible, the timeline for arrival of the new pastor and family should be determined and announced to the congregation.

A Testimony from Ogea

With rare exception, my request to the church and the new pastor is to all for the first Sunday of the new pastor to be the last Sunday of the interim pastor. This special worship service creates an opportunity for me as the interim pastor to preach my last sermon "How to Treat Your New Pastor" (See Appendix J) followed by a New Pastor Installation ceremony (See Appendix K). This arrangement allows the new pastor and family to worship with their new congregation and to join the church as new members. In my three pastorates, I wish that the interim pastor would have gifted me this opportunity of worshipping with my new church family and my family officially joining the church without the pressure of preaching my first sermon my first Sunday.

POSTSCRIPT (OGEA)

PASTORAL TRANSITIONS INTRODUCE a season of change in a congregational context. Some pastoral transitions involve minor change, especially in a healthy congregation. Other pastoral transitions identify major change, generally in churches in need of revitalization. A few pastoral transitions fall in the category of transformational change, requiring radical modifications in the church family system and organizational structure.

My journey has resulted in the completion of seventeen interim pastor assignments. As indicated in the Introduction, some churches experience the blessing of smooth pastoral transitions, while others face the challenge of rough transitions – the result of pastoral leadership failures, including moral failures, unhealthy conflicts, and crisis interruptions. I have experienced all of these situations of rough transitions. Churches experiencing rough transitions, coupled with the need of long-term revitalization, require a time of healing and a refocus toward a new future.

My most recent interim pastor assignment occurred in a downtown First Baptist Church. Upon my arrival, I found a congregation of less than 100 in Sunday morning worship attendance, average age of 72, meeting in a facility with a capacity to accommodate 1200. The church had endured a 40-year decline – yet the remaining members expressed a desire to do "whatever it takes" to revitalize the church and create a new future of growth. Many of them were long-tenured members, who had experienced and survived the decades of decline.

In my first meetings with the Pastor Search Committee, I encouraged and even insisted on crafting a pastor profile that would require the next pastor to be experienced in church revitalization, evangelistic church growth, leadership development, and community outreach. The profile called for a 10-year commitment from the new pastor. Matching this profile with qualifying candidates resulted in a short list, but the PSC persisted, with patience, resulting in the calling of a new pastor who fit their profile. At the writing of this postscript, the new pastor has completed one year, with strong and positive turnaround impact.

I share this case study with the testimony that even the worst of pastoral transition situations can result in strong and positive results. Many of my pastoral transition interims presented themselves as difficult, hard, challenging, and sometimes hopeless situations. I have learned that even the hardest and most hopeless situations can evolve into healthy and victorious outcomes. I have learned that most congregations respond resiliently and faithfully to competent strategic leadership. I have learned that the Lord Jesus is faithful to build His church so that the gates of hell will not overpower it. I have learned that every church deserves the opportunity to survive and thrive instead of decline to the point of death.

I am certainly not an expert in leading churches through pastoral transition. I only hope that this small resource will encourage and challenge pastor search committees, denominational leaders who help churches seeking pastors, and those who serve churches as intentional interims during pastoral transition.

↗

POSTSCRIPT (ECHOLS)

TRANSITIONS IN ANY ORGANIZATION can be the best of times or the worst of times. However, in the church, there need not be a sense of despair, but rather an anticipation of God doing a great work. The stakes are high, but so is the potential reward. The loss of a pastor can bring a new fluidity to previously entrenched positions that resisted change. The fresh winds of the Holy Spirit are ready to blow when a congregation is open to realigning with its true mission.

I have had the privilege of conducting twelve interim pastorates. Numerous challenges faced the churches in those situations. The problems included the need for staff changes and even termination, entrenched leadership that had become complacent, declining attendance, and disunity as well as many other difficulties. However, along with challenges I have seen opportunity. In the three most recent interims that I have done, it took considerable time for the church to become ready for a new pastor. All of them were First Baptist Churches and were in a position to reach and profoundly affect their communities. A unique pastor was needed for each church, all which were different in a number of ways. The process took time. Among the three churches, the shortest amount of time to call a pastor was eleven months. The longest was three years and the other one was twenty-six months. One church was in grave danger of a major split. The other two churches had some significant issues to resolve. In each case, it was evident that the power of prayer, faithful preaching of God's Word, and calling God's people to embrace their mission and to seek a vision from God brought positive change. All three churches are now healthy and have called very capable, dedicated pastors who are just the right fit. Seeing God work through the interim time is a special privilege and blessing.

Just as we need more men to respond to the call to be a pastor, we also desperately need those who will take on the ministry of the transitional interim. Our hope is that this book will encourage more God-called men to come forward to engage in this ministry in a manner that will bear great fruit for His Kingdom!

APPENDIX A

Covenant of Relationship between the Church and the Interim Pastor

This Covenant between ____________ Baptist Church and Dr. Reggie Ogea is entered into to provide clear understandings about relationships and responsibilities necessary to bring glory to God through the growth of the church and the interim pastor throughout the tenure of his ministry.

The church and interim pastor are pleased to enter into this covenant, effective ______________.

A review is to take place every six months during this covenant to determine whether to continue an additional six months. This covenant shall continue in this way until a pastor called by the church has begun his ministry in the church or other conditions make it necessary for the interim/transitional pastor to resign.

Led by the Spirit of God, the Interim Pastor commits to the following:

1. Seek the mind of Christ and the guidance of the Holy Spirit in all things.

2. Be loving and gracious to all and demonstrate a life of integrity in his family, the church, and the community.

3. Be diligent in work according to the work schedule defined below and shared with the church.

4. Use his ministry gifts, knowledge, and wisdom to glorify Christ through the church.

5. Provide spiritual leadership to the church:

    a. Lead Sunday morning worship and preaching

    b. Conduct funerals and bereavement ministry when available.

c. Officiate the ordinance of Baptism when available.

d. Officiate and plan the ordinance of the Lord's Supper with planning worship.

e. Visit the critically ill when available.

f. Meet regularly with the deacons in ministry and be involved with evangelistic visitation Sunday afternoons when available.

g. Provide pastoral counseling or referrals when available.

h. Participate in midweek church activities based on consultation with those organizing.

i. Provide leadership guidance and training for committees and other groups when available.

j. Meet regularly with the Pastor Search Committee and assist the Pastor Search process as a consultant.

k. Represent the church in community, associational, and convention activities as available.

l. Lead additional services, trainings, and prayer meetings when available.

6. Will not be considered as a candidate for the permanent office of pastor.

7. Work with the key leaders and committees as needed to prepare the church for a new pastor.

8. Work cooperatively with ministerial staff and office staff in carrying out the above.

APPENDIX A

Led by the Spirit of God, the Church commits to the following:

1. Be loving and gracious to the interim pastor.

2. Pray for God's Spirit to work in and through the interim pastor's life.

3. Respectfully relate to him as God's anointed leader for this task.

4. Support this leadership with active participation in the church's ministries.

5. Talk with him about personal concerns instead of talking about him to others.

6. Provide a salary and benefits commensurate with the duties of his office as well as mileage (IRS rate), meals, lodging (e.g. a place to go to rest during the day on Sunday), and other expenses as necessary

7. Free the interim pastor to do the work for which he is called as church leaders and members fulfill their ministries.

8. Recognize that the interim pastor's family are faithful members of another church and as such will be limited in their participation in the ministry of ___________ Baptist Church.

9. Plan ahead and let the interim pastor know what committee meetings and events are coming up and discuss with the interim pastor to determine whether the interim pastor's presence is needed and be considerate of the interim pastor's schedule when scheduling meetings and events (e.g. seek to group meetings and events where possible in recognition of the required travel by the interim pastor)

10. Recognize that due to the significant time commitment required, the interim pastor will not be available for weddings.

Work Schedule

The interim pastor commits to spending Sundays on the church field preaching and leading in worship; visiting members and prospects in partnership with the deacons when available, and meeting with church leaders and committees as necessary. Further, the interim pastor plans to participate in midweek services and activities as his schedule allows. The interim pastor will be available in times of crisis at the request of the deacons who will be responsible for ongoing ministry needs.

Salary & Absence

For this part-time position, the Church commits to provide a salary at the rate of ________/year, month, or week to the interim pastor which is commensurate with time spent on the field and in preparation for preaching. Though he will endeavor to avoid absences, some commitments may require occasional absences from the pulpit. In such instances the interim pastor will secure a supply preacher.

This COVENANT OF RELATIONSHIP is entered into by:

____

(Interim Pastor Signature)

____

(Church Representative Signature)

_______/_______/________

Date)

APPENDIX B

How to Get Ready for Your Next Pastor
Hebrews 12:1-3

Thanks for inviting me to worship with you today. I've entitled my sermon today – How to Get Ready for Your Next Pastor. Open your copy of the Bible – God's Word, or view the screens, as we consider Hebrews 12:1-3.

Hebrews 12:1) Therefore, since we also have such a large cloud of witnesses surrounding us, let us lay aside every hindrance and the sin that so easily ensnares us. Let us run with endurance the race that lies before us,

Hebrews 12:2) keeping our eyes on Jesus, the pioneer and perfecter of our faith. For the joy that lay before Him, he endured a cross, despising the shame, and sat down at the right hand of the throne of God.

Hebrews 12:3) For consider Him who endured such hostility from sinners against Himself, so that you won't grow weary and give up.

A Church's Most Challenging Situations. Three situations can be defined as the most challenging in the lifespan of any church:

· A Crisis – Struggling through difficult times, navigating disastrous storms, resolving major conflicts. A crisis will always test the unity and resilience of a congregation.

· A Victory – Opposite a crisis, a victory engages challenges to a church. When a church enjoys a victorious success, the days following an emotional high can be extremely challenging.

· A Major Change – The most challenging congregational situation involves major change, such as the transition from one pastor to the next. You may be the exception, but here's what I've discovered having served as Interim Pastor 16 times: Pastoral transitions potentially define major change in the future of any church.

For this reason, as you begin this journey of transitioning to your next pastor, I challenge you today "How to Get Ready for Your Next Pastor." Some of you might be thinking that this would be better served as a topic for the end of a pastoral transition, not the beginning. I draw your attention back to Hebrews 12 and the end of verse three: "so that you won't grow weary and give up." Two Greek words combine here for a screenshot: Enkakōmen – to grow weary, to lose heart, which leads to Eklyomenoi – to give up, to quit. This combination of words is only used one other time in the NewTestament – Galatians 6:9 Let us not get tired of doing good, for we will reap at the proper time if we don't give up.

This journey could get long and challenging, which could lead to congregational fatigue.

The secret to getting ready for your next pastor requires three looks.

1. LOOK AHEAD – The Race Is Forward! The author of Hebrews defined the Christian life as a race to be run. However, we can make the connection and application of truth to any life-situation as a race to be run. The challenge for us this morning is to view this pastoral transition journey as a race to be run. Verse 1 answers three questions about this race we will run.

"Run the race that lies before us." What kind of race is it? "The race that lies before us." Most of our life-races become marathons instead of sprints. In a sprint, the fastest runner wins and the slowest runner loses. But in a marathon, those who endure to the end finish the race. I must warn you, ________________ Baptist Church, that this race will be a marathon, not a sprint. Remember the challenge: don't grow weary and give up! Remember that even though you don't know at this moment how long you will be without a pastor, God is in control. Remember that God already has your next pastor picked out. Remember that God will meet all of your needs during these days between pastors just as He has always done.

"Run with endurance." How must we run this race? We must run "with endurance." The Greek word is hupomone = "a patient, steadfast waiting for." In a marathon, the runners with endurance and perseverance, cross the finish line. Talk to any marathon runner and they will tell you, that while it would be great to cross the finish line first, the goal of a marathon run is to push through the fatigue, the temptation to quit, and to make it to the finish line. This race of transition set before you will require patience, perseverance, endurance. During these days in transition, everybody needs to be faithful and everybody needs to stay committed. The greatest gift we can give your next pastor is that when he comes, the church is moving forward, not backward. That position will only be possible if you embrace endurance, perseverance, patience.

"Run surrounded by a great cloud of witnesses." Where do we run this race?" "Surrounded by a great cloud of witnesses." As you run, this is not the first time you've run this race and you are not running the race alone. Notice immediately that others have not only run the race, but have finished the race. You are surrounded by a great cloud (nephos) of witnesses. We use the word "cloud" to describe those white, puffy, marsh mellow shapes in the sky. But the Greeks applied "cloud" to describe the highest seats in a stadium. Literally, these words of encouragement remind us that "You're not alone! The grandstands of heaven, all the way up to the clouds – the highest seats in the stadium – are filled with people who have run this race ahead of you!

The greatest challenge of looking forward is to keep your back to the past. Life's tendency tempts us to look back and wonder if the future will repeat the past. You are presented today with a momentary opportunity to change the future trajectory of ______________ Baptist Church.

2. LOOK WITHIN — Examine Your Own Commitment. The things that often hinder us are not outside of us but within us. Sometimes, we are our own worst enemy. What stops us short so often is our own hindrances. It's a personal challenge – each one of you must look within and examine your own commitment. As you look within, two actions were essential:

"Lay aside every hindrance." Onkon = weight or encumbrance. In the first century, athletes wore weights in training for racing events.

Even today, runners sometimes train with weights attached to their ankles. But they wouldn't think of running a race with the weights still attached. When it's time for the race, the weights come off. In the same way, you must lay aside anything and everything that hinders us. What hinders ___________________ Baptist Church from being all that God wants you to be? It starts with you – your attitude, your neglect, your complacency, your resistance to change, your desire for control, your spiritual pride. Each person must be willing to lay aside everything that hinders. Please, I beg you, take this time of transition to pray about your weight, your hindrance, and lay them aside BEFORE your next pastor comes. And remember, what weighs you down impacts the entire congregation.

"Lay aside the sin that so easily ensnares us." The author of Hebrews does not name the sin that so easily ensnare or entangles us. Effective and efficient biblical interpretation always considers context, because context gives us clues. Here, our clue for "the sin that so easily ensnares" is previous chapter. Hebrews 11 is all about faith — the phrase by faith is used twenty-one times in chapter 11. The strong implication is our Faith enables and empowers us to persevere and endure through times of crisis and transition. Since faith enables and empowers us, could it be the lack of faith – unbelief – ensnares and entangles us? Time after time after time, the Bible speaks of people and nations and churches who fell short of victory for one reason and one reason only — lack of faith — unbelief. The amazing thing about unbelief in the life of a Christian is that it tangles up everything else.

And the only one who can do anything about your unbelief is YOU. So, look within — lay aside everything that hinders you and lay aside the sin of unbelief. Examine your own commitment. Don't you be ___________________ Baptist Church's worst enemy.

3. LOOK UP — Keep Your Eyes on Jesus. Aphorontes = a fixation. The only time this word is used in the New Testament describes the goal and attitude of life. Here's one of the greatest texts in all the Bible, exalting Jesus = Perfect Example of Perseverance:

He is the pioneer and perfecter of our faith. He is the originator and finisher of our faith. [Wiersbe, p. 323] He is the Alpha and the Omega — the first and the last. [Revelation 1:17]

He lived the joy set before him. That's an amazing statement. Jesus' life-purpose pointed toward death on the Cross. We call it "good Friday", but for Jesus, Friday was death day on a cross. The amazing thing about Jesus was that for Him the cross defined "the joy set before him." He literally enjoyed doing the will of the Heavenly Father.

He endured a Cross — despising the shame. To be crucified was not only the most painful method of death in the first century, it was also the most shameful - reserved only for the worst of criminals. For the Romans and the Jews to crucify Jesus meant that they thought he was equal to the worst of criminals. In all probability, Jesus was crucified naked, as were all other criminals. How shameful is that!! But in order for Jesus to be our Savior and our Redeemer, he endured the shame and the pain of the Cross — for us!

He has sat down at the right hand of the Father. Jesus received the same glory after completing His assignment that He possessed when He was sent to Earth. The right hand of a King or Ruler is the position of honor. Remember Jesus' disciples arguing about who would have the positions of honor on the right and left of Jesus? Our Lord earned the right to occupy the position of honor because of His endurance.

Notice that the author of Hebrews does not challenge us to look around. Looking around can cause confusion. Looking around can be disappointing. Looking around can misplace focus. Don't look around – look UP.

Beverly King was the richest man in Graham, Texas. He owned the hotel, was a major stockholder and a director at the town bank, and had numerous other business interests. But he seldom dressed or acted the part. Most of the time Beverly King moved around town in his work clothes. One day Mr. King was chitchatting at the car repair shop on the edge of town, when a salesman pulled in with car trouble. The mechanic checked the car, and assured the man he could repair it. However, he would have to order the parts needed and have them delivered the next day. The salesman asked if there was a place to stay in town, and the mechanic pointed to the hotel down the street. It was then that the salesman noticed Mr. King standing off to the side. Thinking he was just a retired town loafer, the salesman asked Mr. King if he would mind carrying his bags to the hotel for him. Mr. King, who had a great sense of humor, played along and said he'd be glad to. As they walked down the street toward the hotel, the salesman said, "As I came into town, I noticed a big house being built on the hill." Mr. King responded, "yes, I've seen it." The salesman said, "That surprises me. I wouldn't think anybody in this town could afford a house like that. Do you know who it belongs to?" Mr. King answered, "Yes, it belongs to me." The salesman was stunned. "It belongs to you? How in the world can you afford a house like that? Mr. King quietly answered as he kept walking, "Because —all of these years, I've carried my own bags." [Told by Paul Powell in *Getting the Lead Out of Leadership*, pp. 103-104]

During these days of transition, each and every one of you must determine to CARRY YOUR OWN BAGS – pull your own weight – fulfill your responsibilities. Look ahead – the race is forward. Look within – examine your own commitment. And Look Up – Keep your eyes on Jesus! Embrace these three looks, so that you won't grow weary and give up.

APPENDIX C

A Door Set Open
Revelation 3:7-8

Revelation 3:7) Write to the angel of the church in Philadelphia: "Thus says the Holy One, the true one, the one who has the key of David, who opens and no one will close, and who closes and no one opens:

Revelation 3:8) I know your works. Look, I have placed before you an open door that no one can close because you have but little power; yet you have kept my word and have not denied my name."

Our biblical text this morning contains the message of Jesus Christ, the risen, resurrected Messiah, to the apostle John, who was exiled on Patmos, a small, secluded island in the Mediterranean Sea. John is the only one of the original of Jesus' twelve disciples alive. As John looked across the Sea, separated from his biological family and his church family, despair and discouragement overwhelmed him. In that context, Jesus allowed John to see and experience an apokalupsis, (Apocalypse) literally "an unveiling" – a panoramic view of the future – a message of hope, that the future is in God's hands, and the best is yet to be. God has always been in control and the future is in His hands. The Resurrected Jesus commands John to write what he see, what is, and what will take place after this. (Revelation 1:19)

A wealthy businessman took a day off to hike in a national park. He just wanted to clear his head and enjoy the aloneness of a day in the park. Unfortunately, he got lost. When he didn't come home, they searched the park and found his abandoned truck. The next morning, the park rangers launched an immediate search and rescue. On the third day, a park ranger spotted him in a remote area of the park, far from any trail or campsite. The lost businessman was incoherent, dehydrated, exhausted, and dazed. The park ranger asked him, "Sir, how did you get here and where were you going?" Verifying that he in fact was the lost businessman, the park ranger led him back to safety.

After a brief stay in the hospital, the businessman returned to work and immediately called the park, asking for the identity of the park ranger who rescued him. He made an appointment with the ranger and offered him a job, with compensation much higher than his annual pay as a ranger. The park ranger was a stunned: "Why do you want me to work for you? You don't know me. All I've ever been is a park ranger. What can I possible do for you in your business?" The businessman replied, "Ever since you found me in the park, I can't get out of my mind the two questions you asked me – How did you get here and where were you going? I want you to come work for me and every morning, I want you to ask me those two questions: How did you get here and where are you going? I want those two questions to mark every day for the rest of my life."

Today marks the beginning of our journey during these days and months of transition. I propose these **Two Questions for a New Beginning: How Did We Get Here? Where Do We Go From Here?** My role as your Transitional Pastor is simply to Preach Well and Lead Well – reasonable expectations. In my first sermon back on February 5th, I challenged you to take three looks – look ahead (a forward look), look within (a frank look), and look up (a future look) – also reasonable expectations. I cannot predict nor see the specific outcome of this journey toward your next pastor, but I can predict and see a successful outcome if together, we embrace these reasonable expectations.

This apocalupsis that John sees unfolds with messages to seven churches. In the message to the church in Philadelphia (the church of brotherly love), John heard these encouraging words: "Thus says the Holy One, the true one, the one who has the key of David, who opens and no one will close, and who closes and no one opens: I know your works. Look, I have placed before you an open door that no one can close. I can just hear a similar message to __________________ Baptist Church: God knows our works. God agonizes with our past. God identifies with our present. And God sees our future. The omniscient, all-knowing God has positioned us before a door set open. As we stand before our door set open, may I challenge us in this new beginning to consider two Responses.

Accept the Reality of the Present. The Philadelphia church endured hard and difficult times. Jesus commended them: "Because you have kept my command to endure, I will also keep you from the hour of testing that is going to come on the whole world to test those who live on the earth." (Rev. 3:10) Hard times, tough times, disappointing times require endurance. Hard times, tough times, disappointing times are testing times. James declared a strange response to testing – "Consider it great joy, my brothers and sisters, whenever you experience various trials, because you know that the texting of your faith produces endurance." (James 1:2-3)

The Present Looks Back to the Past in order to Reclaim a Strong Heritage. The danger of looking back to the past often opines a wishful redo or reset. Ed Stetzer once exclaimed, "If we could go back to the 1950s, Southern Baptist churches are ready!" The problem with a wishful redo or reset is that it can never happen. Tradition and heritage must be celebrated, but

To Reclaim a Strong Heritage Requires Accepting Reality instead of Alternate Reality. I think you know instinctively that ________________ Baptist Church cannot go back to relive the past. We must look back to reclaim a glorious heritage, and that heritage will look much different in the future. For many of us in our senior years, and that's most of us here today, we drift into the mentality that the church exists for us, to meet our needs, to minister to our situations. The church should do all of that, but if we only see the church as existing for us, we neglect that the church exists also for those who are not here yet – for those yet to be reached. We must not selfishly hold onto a church that will exist for us – we must recreate, revision, and rebirth a church that will reach the generation of our grandchildren.

As we stand before a door set open, we not only accept the reality of the present, but we must also Activate a Hope for the Future. Of the seven Revelation churches, the Philadelphia church is the only one who did not receive a warning from the risen Jesus. Instead they were challenged to "hold onto what you have so that no one takes your crown. The one who conquers I will make a pillar in the temple of my God, and he will never go out again. I will write on him the name of my God and the name of the city of my God – new Jerusalem, which comes down out of heaven from my God – and my new name." This church could embrace a new hope – a new angle of vision. I'm challenging us to shift our stance this morning – let's

Stand with Our Back to the Past Facing the Future. Let's allow hope to carry us over the threshold of "there's nothing we can do to change our future." I'm going to ask you to do something unique this morning. Could we agree that we will remove the word "impossible" from our vocabulary? Can we lock arms and minds and hearts together in unity, and believe that "nothing is impossible with God?" Will you join me today on a new adventure – a new beginning as we stand with our backs to the past facing the future.

However, before you say, "I'm all in" – let me warn you that The Future Requires Change and Courage. Peter Steinke proposed that "Change is a magnet for emotional reactions. Anxiety becomes more intense. Highly agitated anxiety produces excessive apprehension." (A Door Set Open, page 21). An Old Testament example encourages us. Nehemiah proposed a vision for the people of Israel, rebuilding the wall of Jerusalem with a shield of brick and stone. Immediately, Sanballat launched a mean-spirited attack on Nehemiah's vision of change, accusing him of seditious and prideful activity, inciting doubt and fear among the people. But Nehemiah stayed the course, kept his eyes on the completed task, stood on his principles, and tapped into God's strength. When the threat came, Nehemiah asked, "Should a man like me run away?" He did not run, and the wall was completed in 52 days! (Nehemiah 6:11-15) Transformational change, adaptive change, even systemic change requires courage – it is no easy process. And it is always painful. But without pain there is no gain.

Change demands courage. No crisis destroys a church, only the lack of response to the crisis. ________________ Baptist Churhc, you are not today what you used to be. I commend you for staying here through difficult days. Thank you for not leaving. Thanks for not running from the fire. No disrespect for those who leave in the midst of conflict, but it's easier to leave than to stay and deal with the conflict. Now that you've stayed, what you do next will determine your future.

As your Interim Pastor, I do not bring with me a magical formula. However, this will be my 17th time to serve a church as Interim Pastor. I make you this promise – if you will stay committed and unified, if you will accept reality and activate hope, if you will pray as if it all depended on God and work as if it all depended on you, if you will expect great things from God while you attempt great things for God, then the day will come when we can sing "To God Be the Glory, Great things He hath done."

Conclusion

Look, I have placed before you an open door that no one can close.

_________________ Baptist Church – Do you see it? Will you accept the reality of the present: How did we get here? If we accept the reality of our present, we must reject any and all false notions and alternate realities. We must accept the truth of where we find ourselves right now.

Will you activate a hope for the future: Where do we go from here? If we activate our hope in the future, we must stand with our backs to the past and we must face a future of change and courage.

What do you say? Are you ready? Let's go!

APPENDIX D

Prayer Emphasis for Pastor Search

Developed by the Staff of First Baptist Church, Vidalia, Georgia

I. Pray for our own relationship with the Lord

- Read the Lord's Prayer: Matthew 6: 9-13 Note the elements of:

Praise
Petition
Pardon
Protection

2. Pray for the church to be ready for the leadership of the pastor

- Pray that our church will be humbled to seek the Lord
- Pray that our church will be united in its fellowship, and its service to the Lord
- Pray that our church will be faithful to its mission during the time of the search for the pastor
- Pray for lost souls to be saved through the ministry of our church during the interim

3. Prayer for members of the Pastor Search Team

- Blessings and grace for the search team members and their families as much time will be required
- Ability to maintain confidentiality
- Unity of spirit and mind - pray daily for one another
- Anointing of God's Spirit to see from His perspective what He wants for His church
- Seeking God daily for wisdom, a word, and encouragement for others.
- Stand on God's word, His promises
- Ability to wait on God and not rush nor slow the process
- That they do not grow weary in the waiting or be premature in selection

- Freedom/boldness to speak up (each member matters by divine appointment)
- Being careful and considerate of well-meaning individuals who may pressure or try to influence
- Wisdom and discernment in looking at resumes/candidates
- Ability to see beyond the page/interview to discover character and gifts as well as weaknesses
- Ability to communicate with the body that God is at work and what your prayer needs are

4. Prayers for our next Pastor

- Pray God is working in the heart of our next pastor to prepare him and his family for this ministry at FBCV
- Pray for the ministry he may be leaving that God will fill that void to His glory in His time
- Pray for his wife and family as they prepare for this transition to new things

CHURCH LEADER SURVEY
FBC Lafayette, LA

Your Pastor Search Committee would like for you to give this matter your prayerful and thoughtful attention. You are the church. We want your suggestions and recommendations in regards to the selection of a pastor. This will help in the work you have asked us to do.

How much pastoral experience should our new pastor have?

☐ Under 5 years
☐ 5-10 years
☐ 10-20 years
☐ Over 20 years

While age should not be the primary factor, approximately what age pastor do you feel our church should have at this time?

☐ 20-30
☐ 30-40
☐ 40-50
☐ 50-55
☐ 55-60

What educational qualifications should our new pastor have?

☐ High School
☐ College degree
☐ Some seminary training
☐ Seminary degree
☐ Post-graduate work
☐ Other

A pastor has many important responsibilities. While he ought to be interested in each of the following, which do you feel should receive most of his time? (check five)

☐ Visiting prospective members
☐ Sermon preparation
☐ Administration and office work
☐ Counseling and advising
☐ Personal Bible study and prayer
☐ Personal witnessing
☐ Visiting church members

☐ Civic affairs
☐ Promoting church ministries
☐ Attending meetings
☐ Caring for the needs of his own family
☐ Attending denominational meetings

On which of these should he spend the least amount of time? (List two)

What do you feel is the most important quality our pastor should possess? Feel free to express your feelings about other characteristics you would like to have in a pastor.

Other Characteristics

Additional Comments:

APPENDIX F

PASTOR SEARCH
CONGREGATIONAL SURVEY

must be submitted by July 18

Please return completed surveys to the Welcome Center located in the entrance lobby of the Worship Center. Surveys will be collected until after the worship service on July 18th. An electronic version of this survey is available by scanning the QR ink to the left. Your answers to this survey are anonymous and will only be viewed by those involved in the pastor-search process.

ABOUT YOU

(1) What is your gender?

- ☐ Male
- ☐ Female

(2) What is your current age?

- ☐ Under 12
- ☐ 12-17
- ☐ 18-29
- ☐ 30-39
- ☐ 40-49
- ☐ 50-59
- ☐ 60-69
- ☐ 70 or more

(3) What is your marital status?

- ☐ Never married
- ☐ Currently married
- ☐ Separated or divorced
- ☐ Widowed

(4) Do you have children under eighteen living at home?

- ☐ Yes
- ☐ No

(5) Are you a church member?

- ☐ Yes
- ☐ No

(6) Circle the number that best describes your involvement:

1 2 3 4 5

not very active ⟵⟶ very active

APPENDIX F

SURVEY

Please answer the following questions to indicate your expectations for our church's next pastor.

(7) What is the desired age range for the pastor?
(choose **one**)

- ☐ <35
- ☐ 35-45
- ☐ 46-55
- ☐ 56 or more
- ☐ No age preference

(8) What is the minimal acceptable educational level you expect the next pastor to have attained?
(choose **one**)

- ☐ College graduate (bachelor's degree)
- ☐ Master's degree from seminary
- ☐ Doctoral degree from seminary
- ☐ Formal education degree not important

(9) What pastoral or professional ministry experience should be required?
(choose **one**)

- ☐ Less than 5 years of prior experience as pastor
- ☐ At least 5 years of prior experience as pastor
- ☐ Ten years or more prior experience as pastor
- ☐ Doesn't matter

(10) What should the size of the prospective pastor's current church be in relation to our church?
(choose **one**)

- ☐ Somewhat larger than our church
- ☐ Somewhat smaller than our church
- ☐ About the same size as our church
- ☐ Doesn't matter

(11) Rank the following by order of importance you would expect of a prospective pastor?
(1-most; 5-least)

___ Preaching/Teaching
___ Administration
___ Pastoral Care
___ Strategic Leadership
___ Community Involvement

FIRST BAPTIST CHURCH OF KENNER
page 2

SURVEY

continued...

(12) The following are activities to which a pastor may allocate time each week. Choose the top 3 areas that should be the priorities of our new pastor.
(choose **three**)

- ☐ Administration, including tasks related to the church office, finances, and facility
- ☐ Correspondence with members by phone, e-mail, and social media
- ☐ Counseling individuals with personal and spiritual problems
- ☐ Evangelistic outreach
- ☐ Casting vision with church staff, deacons, and ministry leaders
- ☐ Sermon preparation
- ☐ Prayer
- ☐ Attending social gatherings and special events of ministries, classes, and groups in
- ☐ Planning and organizing ministry activities
- ☐ Other (please specify):

(13) Compared to our church's current worship services, would you want the prospective pastor to lead in making any of the following changes?
(choose **one**)

- ☐ Include more traditional elements
- ☐ Include more contemporary elements
- ☐ Use more blended elements
- ☐ No change to current worship services
- ☐ Other (please specify):

(14) Which of the following preaching styles most effectively communicate to you?
(choose **three**)

- ☐ Narrative (use of stories to illustrate points)
- ☐ Personal, relational, engaging
- ☐ Expository (preaching directly from a particular text/passage)
- ☐ Sermon series (spending multiple weeks on a Bible book)
- ☐ Social action (appealing for action or change)
- ☐ Verse by verse through a text
- ☐ Bible book (multiple weeks on a Bible book)

FIRST BAPTIST CHURCH OF KENNER
page 3

APPENDIX F

SURVEY
continued...

(15) Of the ministry priorities in our church, which five below does the incoming pastor need to emphasize most?
(choose **five**)

- ☐ Discipleship and spiritual formation
- ☐ Developing small Bible study groups/classes
- ☐ Helping the congregation build healthy relationships
- ☐ Evangelism and showing Jesus through word and action
- ☐ Leadership, vision and formulating a plan for the future of the church
- ☐ Care for the needy (social compassion)
- ☐ Denominational involvement including the Cooperative Program
- ☐ Missions involvement
- ☐ Prayer and prayer ministry
- ☐ Organizing new ministries and empowering leaders for ministry
- ☐ Understanding the context of our local community
- ☐ Corporate and personal worship
- ☐ Strengthening families
- ☐ Outreach (increasing our numbers)

(16) What keeps you as a part of this congregation?

(17) What do you see as the greatest need for our church at this time?

(18) Is there anything else you'd like us to know?

RETURN SURVEY TO WELCOME CENTER IN THE WORSHIP CENTER BY JULY 18

APPENDIX G

First Baptist Church of Baton Rouge
Senior Pastor Search Notice

June 1, 2023

First Baptist Church (FBC) of Baton Rouge is a fellowship of believers who love the Lord and his Word. Teaching is centered on the Bible, and there is a loving atmosphere.

FBC has been a feature in downtown Baton Rouge for 149 years. It has planted dozens of churches throughout the greater community. Our church has a reputation for the excellence of its music ministry, often utilizing instrumentalists from the LSU School of Music.

About twenty years ago, FBC opened a second campus in suburban Baton Rouge. That facility operated as part of FBC until 2009 when it was granted mission church status. The combined worship attendance at both locations prior to 2009 was approximately 450. Afterwards, the in-person worship attendance downtown averaged around 225 until the COVID closures in 2020. We are currently building back near those levels. An average of 25 viewers watches the live stream of the worship service. Sunday School attendance averaged around 180 prior to COVID. We have not gotten back to that level but we are seeing positive increases.

The FBC congregation is aging, as are most churches. The number of families with young children is the lowest percentage it has ever been. Fortunately, Baton Rouge is a relatively young city. With two universities, many young adults choose to stay, and many are unchurched. An additional opportunity is that residential condominiums and apartments are being built downtown near the church.

Baton Rouge is ethnically diverse, with large African American and Hispanic populations. Our worship attendance is not ethnically diverse, but FBCBR is open to outreach to all.

Our budget has been running about $1.3 million. We have a large physical plant including an iconic sanctuary and no debt.

FBC is excited about the next phase of its journey to fulfill the Great Commission and glorify God.

OUR NEIGHBORHOOD

FBC is in downtown Baton Rouge. A 2023 demographics report from the North American Mission Board revealed the following about the three-mile radius around the church. The population is about 58,000 of which 34,000 are Millennials and Gen Z's. The median household has 2.2 people with a household income of $40,000. The median age is 30 with roughly 10,000 children in the area. About 36% of adults in the area have college degrees. Roughly half are registered Democrat and about 15% are Republican. About 40% attend church with any regularity. The crime index is 219 with 100 being average.

Downtown Baton Rouge and the area south of downtown near the LSU campus have experienced sustained redevelopment over the past 25 years. LSU is in the three-mile radius of the church. Condominiums and apartments have become the preferred residences for students over dormitories, and numerous complexes have been built to accommodate them. Several are located between the campus and church.

There has also been a trend toward construction of new apartments and condos in downtown proper. The Heron apartment complex was recently completed and is being rented up adjacent to the church on its east side. This is a six-story luxury complex with 142 units, parking garage, pool and gym. The 21 story Chase Tower at the northwest corner of the church is being redeveloped with conversion of most of its office space to 150 luxury apartments.

There are more than 3,000 apartments in downtown Baton Rouge, a full-size grocery store, pharmacy and numerous restaurants. Large Catholic, Episcopal, Presbyterian and Baptist churches are downtown. The neighborhood has become somewhat self-contained and viable for those seeking to live in the city center.

Most of the membership of our church resides more than three miles to the southeast of the church. Our challenge, and the challenge for our next pastor, is to find ways to attract and reach new downtown residents and American and international college students, our neighbors, for Christ.

NEIGHBORHOOD MAP

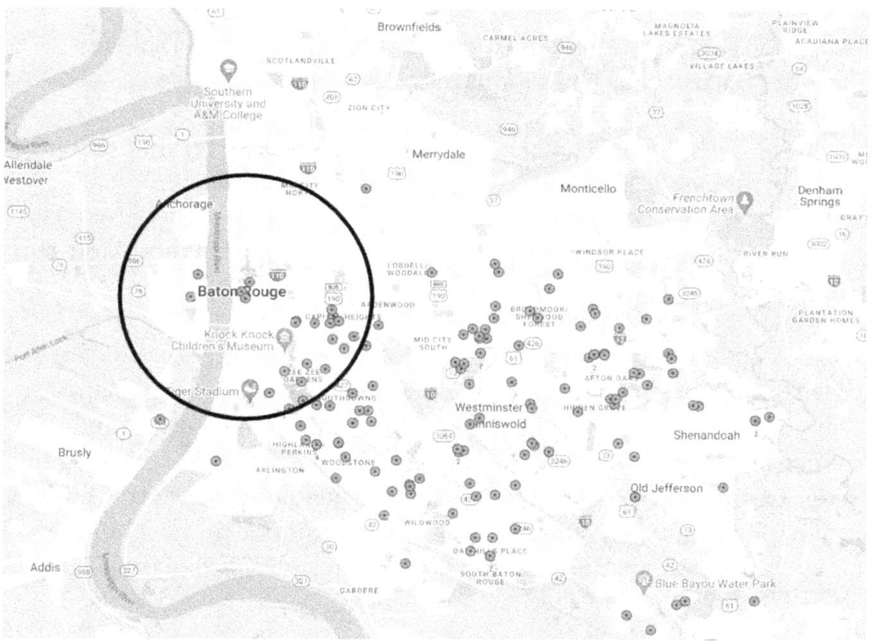

Neighborhood Map Showing Three Mile Radius
and Member Residence Locations

PASTOR PROFILE

First Baptist Church of Baton Rouge, Louisiana invites applications for the position of Full Time Senior Pastor. We are a biblically sound Southern Baptist congregation with a long history and great potential for the future.

APPENDIX G

We are prayerfully seeking God's will for selecting our next Senior Pastor. The candidate must be committed to the inerrancy and authority of the Scripture, agree with the Baptist and Faith Message 2000 and passionately lead the Church in fulfilling the Great Commission and proclaiming the message of the Gospel of Jesus Christ. He must walk in Biblical truth, promote Christ-centric relationships, possess spiritual maturity, foster compassionate ministry, and live in joyful obedience.

We prefer a candidate who has ten years plus experience as a Senior Pastor or one who has had significant pastoral leadership experience.

We prefer a candidate who has successfully led a church revitalization effort or who has seen sustained growth under his leadership.

A seminar degree is required with preference from a Southern Baptist Seminary. A Doctor of Ministry or PhD is a plus, but not required.

We believe the man God calls as the next Senior Pastor of First Baptist Church Baton Rouge should possess and exhibit competence in and commitment to the following key areas of ministry. If after reviewing this Senor Pastor Profile and after prayerful consideration, the Lord leads you to submit a resume for consideration by the Pastor Search Committee, please submit your resume to: FBCBRpastorresume@gmail.com.

Preaching and Teaching of Scripture

- Prepare and Preach Scripture-based sermons centered on personal Bible study and prayer with relevant personal applications.
- Preach the Word with boldness in a clear and understanding manner while challenging the congregation to action.
- Encourage various styles of worship and Bible study in a variety of settings to reach all generations with emphasis on young families, youth and children.
- Lead, promote and grow a vibrant Sunday School Program across all age groups and life stages.

Outreach and missions

- Exhibit a passion and commitment to reach those in our city and surrounding areas through innovative methods, leveraging technology, including computer and media-to further Christ's work in the Church and in the community.
- Encourage domestic and international missions to reach those who have yet to come to faith in Jesus Christ.
- Consistently share and encourage others to share the message of the Gospel with those with whom they come in contact.
- Personally witness and lead church visitation and outreach.
- Focus on fostering a church that welcomes, ministers and disciples all walks of life, generations and cultural backgrounds in order to share the Gospel and grow the Church.
- Support the Cooperative Program through the Louisiana Baptist Convention.

Vision and Leadership

- Be a gentle spirit, above reproach, humble, sober and a good husband (and if applicable father) to his family.
- Be a role model for individual and corporate prayer and Bible study.
- Be a good listener, counselor and have a genuine concern for the care of the congregation and the community.
- Be a person able to inspire and motivate the congregation to join in God's vision for growing First Baptist Church.
- Be the face of First Baptist Church in the downtown community through media, social media and participation in civic organizations to expand the reach of the Church ministries.
- Be an effective leader in setting the vision and strategy in all aspects of the Church's activities.
- Lead staff through mentoring and development.
- Encourage, inspire and motivate church members and lay membership to minister as Christ's Heart, Hands and Feet through their spiritual gifts and talents.
- Nurture activities and interaction across generations to treasure our past and embrace our future.

APPENDIX H

FBC Baton Rouge Pastor Search Committee

Initial Candidate Ranking Sheet

Candidate Name	Preaching Rank (1)	Overall Rank (2)

(1) After prayerful consideration and the leading of the Holy Spirit and having watched at least two video sermons of each candidate, please rank each candidate from 1 to 5 based on your assessment of the quality, effectiveness and overall strength of his preaching as compared to each of the other four candidates. Please rank your top candidate based on preaching alone as 1, your next candidate based on preaching alone as 2 and so on from 1 to 5. Do not rank any candidates with the same ranking.

(2) After prayerful consideration and the leading of the Holy Spirit, please rank each candidate from 1 to 5 based on your overall assessment of the strength of the candidate as compared to each of the other four candidates. This ranking should not only take into account the preaching rank for the applicable candidate but also your overall view of the strength of the candidate based on his education, experience and other attributes deemed important for a viable candidate based on the congregational Senior Pastor Profile. Please rank your top overall candidate as 1, your next overall candidate as 2 and so on from 1 to 5. Do not rank any candidates with the same ranking.

APPENDIX I

Prospective Pastor Questionnaire, FBCBR

Questions of Common Agreement:

Please describe your conversion experience and your call to ministry.

Describe your personal devotional practices.

What are some examples of God's unique ways He prepared you for ministry? Can you name some job experiences, life experiences, and/or suffering experiences that God used to give you a unique perspective on ministry?

What are your lead spiritual gifts and how do you put them into practice? How do your spiritual gifts, education, ministry experience, and skills enable you to serve as pastor of a local church?

Do you agree with/subscribe to the 2000 Baptist Faith and Message statement as adopted by the Southern Baptist Convention? Are there any elements in or not in the Baptist Faith and Message that you would like to expand upon?

Share your vision related to the Cooperative Program of the Southern Baptist Convention. Please share the level of Cooperative Program participation in the church you now (or recently) serve as pastor.

Describe your preaching style. What is your philosophy of preaching? What is your hermeneutical approach?

What do you see as the most important tasks of a Pastor? Please list them in the order of importance to you.

Who are some of the theologians, pastors, professors, or authors who have shaped your theology? In addition to the Bible, what three books have you read recently?

APPENDIX I

Please describe any faith-based organizations, conferences or websites that you occasionally use as resources?

Please explain your views on worship style for today's church considering our culture.

What is your view of Calvinism?

Did Jesus die for everyone?

Is election conditional or unconditional?

What is your view of church polity and the role of deacons vs. elders?

Describe your leadership style as it applies to the church body, the deacon body, and other staff.

Do you believe in tithing and do you practice tithing?

Individual Questions

What is your practice of pastoral visitation?

How do you approach delegation?

What is your view of the role of activities outside of church life such as the SBC, state conventions, or community organizations such as civic clubs or chambers of commerce?

Describe the top priorities in your life that require your time now and in the foreseeable future? How do you balance your family life with your duties at church?

What is the role and involvement of your wife in your ministry.

What is your strategy for personal witnessing?

APPENDIX I

What are some ideas that you implemented in your former church that you would like to implement in our church? What are some ideas that you were unable to implement in a former church that you would like to implement in our church?

Have you ever been dismissed by vote of the congregation from employment of any church (this question does not imply you were at fault). If yes, please explain.

Have employees, staff, church members, or others with whom you worked with ever brought charges of sexual harassment against you before either a church body or any civil governmental agency or court? If yes, please explain.

Are you currently under continuing medical care for any condition that would affect your ability to carry out a pastor's responsibilities or duties?

YES/NO QUESTIONS

Do you believe in "same-sex marriage?

Do you believe the Bible has the answers to life's problems?

Do you think it is biblical to have women pastors leading a church?

Is there an exception clause that would allow an abortion by the mother?

Do you believe the Bible teaches a literal Hell?

Do you believe the Bible teaches that believers should have a private prayer language by speaking in tongues?

Do you believe in the literal return of Jesus Christ to planet Earth?

Do you believe that Mormons' and Jehovah's Witnesses' views on Jesus Christ are the same as Baptists'?

Do you believe in tithing (10% of your income), and do you practice it?

APPENDIX J

How to Treat Your New Pastor
1 Peter 5:1-4

1 Peter 5:1) I exhort the elders among you as a fellow elder and witness to the sufferings of Christ, as well as one who shares in the glory about to be revealed:

1 Peter 5;2) Shepherd God's flock among you, not overseeing out of compulsion but willingly, as God would have you; not out of greed for money but eagerly; 3) not lording it over those entrusted to you, but being examples to the flock. 4) And when the chief Shepherd appears, you will receive the unfading crown of glory.

This morning is a new day in the life of First Baptist Church Baton Rouge. After a long journey, you have the joy of welcoming your new pastor, Dr. Andrew Ogea. In their first interview with Andrew, the Pastor Search Committee probed his knowledge of the Bible by asking him to interpret for them his favorite Bible story. In response, Andrew shared with them his understanding of the parable of the Good Samaritan.

"There was a Good Samaritan traveling from Jerusalem to Jericho and he fell among thorns, which sprang up and choked him and left him half dead. As he lay there, the Queen of Sheba rode by in her chariot, and after tending to his wounds, loaded the Good Samaritan and off they went. As they rode along the road, the Good Samaritan began to feel better. He stood up, and his hair got caught in the branches of a juniper tree. He hung there for forty days and forty nights, and the ravens came and fed him. After hanging there, Delilah came along and cut off his hair and he fell on stony ground. He said – I will arise – and he arose and off in the distance he saw the tower of Babel. As he approached the tower, Jezebel walked out on the balcony in her robe of many colors. When she noticed the Good Samaritan, she began to mock him. He called out to those with her – "Throw her down". And they threw her down seventy-times seven, and of the fragments they picked up twelve baskets full. Now the question is: "Whose wife will she be on the day of judgment."

Well, needless to say, the Pastor Search Committee sat there speechless. Finally, John Lizana spoke up: "I've heard enough. We don't need to go any further. It's obvious that Bro. Andrew sure knows his Bible. I make a motion we call him as our pastor!"

Now, before we go any further, and for those of you who think that's the way the parable of the Good Samaritan goes, I have to tell you I made that up! That really didn't happen with Andrew. But John? Seriously, I do want you to know excited and elated Vicki and I feel for you and for our son and his precious family. I am confident that this is going to be a great journey between pastor and people. One of the tasks I've tried to do as your Interim Pastor is to prepare you for the great future you have before you. God has positioned you for such a time as this. You have weathered the storm and revitalized your future. You embrace a tremendous opportunity to get to the next level and to become a great church again.

So, I want to encourage you today as you welcome your new pastor and his family. Many factors converge into a successful relationship between pastor and people, but to a great degree, much of life comes down to how we treat one another. For the time we have left this morning, I want to discuss with you How to Treat Your New Pastor.

In 1 Peter 5, Simon Peter merged three biblical words to define and describe the function of pastor. It's the only place in the New Testament where all three of these words are spoken in the same text.

Elder = Leader. Peter challenged the elders (presbyteroi), a word used throughout the New Testament identifying those who held leadership positions in the church. In 2 Corinthians 10:3-5 the Apostle Paul reminded the Corinthian Christians that though we live in the world, we do not wage war as the world does. The weapons we fight with are not weapons of the world. On the contrary, we possess divine power to demolish strongholds. And in Ephesians 6, Paul challenged believers to put on the armor of God and arm themselves with the sword of the Spirit in order to fight against the strategies of Satan. This imagery positioned the church as the army of God, and all of us know that an army needs a leader, a general, someone to lead from the front. Pastors are leaders who lead from the front. Andrew is coming here to be your leader.

Pastor = Shepherd. As a fellow elder (a sympresbyteros) Peter challenged the presbyteroi to shepherd God flock among you (poimaino). The noun form of this verb is poimen, the word often translated pastor. A pastor is a shepherd – one who tends the flock. Jesus' favorite designation for the church was the flock of God. Shepherds function as guardians, leaders, protectors, comforters, and at times rescuers of God's flock. Andrew is coming here to be your shepherd.

Overseer = Manager. Peter's third descriptor is the word episkopoi – overseers – sometimes translated bishop. A pastor is not only a respected leader and shepherd, but also an overseer – a manager.
In addition to being the army of God and the flock of God, the New Testament defined the church as the family of God. 1 Timothy 3 lists the character qualities of a pastor/overseer, and one of those descriptors is that he is "one who manages his own household competently, having his children under control with all dignity. If anyone does not know how to manage his own household, how will he take care of God's church? (1 Timothy 3:4) Andrew is coming here to be your overseer.

For my last sermon, utilizing these three biblical designations, I urge and implore you to embrace three attitudes and treat your new pastor this way. I give credit to Jackie Kay, one of our finest SBC Evangelists, for this outline.

HELP HIM, DON'T HOUND HIM. Let me tell you a secret about my son Andrew: He's only one man. He is not superman – he is not faster than a speeding bullet, he is not more powerful than a locomotive, he is not able to leap tall buildings in a single bound. He does not have all power – he can only be one place at a time – he is not a mind-reader. He cannot possibly do everything that needs to be done in this church. If he is going to function effectively and efficiently as shepherd, overseer, and leader, he is going to need everybody's help.

APPENDIX J

A Pastor's Success = sum total of Everybody's help. If you want him to be one of the finest pastors in the history of First Baptist Baton Rouge, then every one of you must stand with him, alongside of him, and behind him to help him, and not hound him.

HEAR HIM OUT, DON'T HUSH HIM UP. Dr. Ogea will do many things as your new pastor. He will plan and lead worship services. He will counsel with people. He will supervise the church staff. He will attend meetings. He will participate in all kinds of visitation. He will share Jesus with those spiritually lost and personally unchurched. He will marry people and he will bury people. However,

A Pastor's most important Responsibility = Preach God's Word. To preach effectively, week after week, will demand his time in prayer, in Bible study, and in seeking God's will for the church. How well he preaches God's Word will impact the effectiveness of all other pastoral duties. Sometimes that means that he will have to stand here and deliver a message that may be difficult and hard to bear. Sometimes he will stand here with a burden on his heart. At all times he is required to preach the whole counsel of God. Sometimes you will think that he is preaching directly to you. Sometimes, his message will not be popular.

A pastor stood one Sunday morning with a bandage on his chin. Before beginning his sermon, he explained his injury. He said, "I had my mind on my sermon this morning while shaving and cut my chin." When the worship service ended, a church member was overheard saying, "He should have kept his mind on his chin and cut the sermon." You may feel that way sometimes. But listen to how the Bible defines a Pastor's Preaching Obligation: 2 Timothy 4:2 -- "Proclaim the message; persist in it whether convenient or not; rebuke, correct, and encourage with great patience and teaching." Your pastor is charged to preach, to deliver the Word, when you're ready to hear it and when you're not ready to hear it; when it's easy and when it is hard. Sometimes his message will be a rebuke, sometimes a correction, sometimes an encouragement. Regardless, it is your responsibility to hear him out, not hush him up.

APPENDIX J

HUG HIM, DON'T HURT HIM.

One special gift your new pastor will always need, and everyone of you can give it to him. I've already shared with you two special gifts you can give your new pastor: keeping the church moving forward and praying constantly. Now here's another special gift:

A Pastor's greatest Need = Encouragement. 2 Chronicles 15 records that the Spirit of God anointed a prophet named Azariah as he observed King Asa lead Judah in a season of renewal, calling the people to trust completely in the Lord. Azariah's inspired word for Asa is one of the great lines of encouragement in the Old Testament: "But as for you, be strong; don't give up, for your work has a reward. (2 Chronicles 15:9) Azariah's words, "Don't give up" translate a Hebrew phrase that means literally, "Don't let your hands drop." What a powerful picture of discouragement. When our hands drop, we are no longer getting the work done, and we open ourselves to the enemy's knockout punch.

The greatest threat to your new pastor is not moral disqualification, nor is it theological error. Some pastors are forced from their ministry positions for these reasons, but not most. Most who let their hands drop from the work do so because they give up, they lose courage, they grow weary and lose heart. An encouraging word can make all the difference. Your new pastor's going to have enough pressure and stress. He's going to have more than he can do. He will never get caught up. He will never please everybody. In fact, if Andrew Ogea would try to please everybody, he would end up pleasing nobody. His first priority is husband to Amy and father to Macy, Ellie, and Caleb. He won't be a great pastor if he is not first a great husband and father. He is married to Amy – he is not married to First Baptist Church. First Baptist Baton Rouge is the Bride of Christ, not the bride of the Andrew Ogea. For him to be everything he must be and do everything he must do, he will need all of the encouragement you can give him.

So hug him, don't hurt him. He needs your prayers – not your gossip. He needs your kindness – not your criticism. He needs your love – not your complaints. He needs your forgiveness – not your harshness. He needs your understanding – not your murmuring. And remember, what you do to him is magnified within his family. If you hurt him, your will hurt his family deeper.

I leave you with one last thought: Dr. Andrew Ogea = Committed to NEXT. A Pastor's Effectiveness is marked by his willingness and courage to do what must be done NEXT! Dr. Andrew Ogea is committed to NEXT! He and his family have determined that next for them is First Baptist Baton Rouge. Today is the beginning of a new journey for both pastor and people. It all comes down to attitude. I know very well the heart of Andrew, Amy, Macy, Ellie, and Caleb. They want to do their best. They are moving here because they are convinced it is God's will. They are excited. They are committed. They will work hard. They will labor long. They may lead you to the greatest days this church experienced in a long, long time. It can happen, if you will pledge today to help them instead of hounding them, to hear them out instead of hushing them up, and to hug them instead of hurting them.

This is the sermon I preached at First Baptist Church, Baton Rouge, LA, the day my son, Dr. Andrew Ogea, was installed as pastor, June 16, 2024. It was a very surreal experience to have my son to be the chosen pastor. When the PSC determined that they wanted to consider Andrew, I withdrew my presence from all their meetings as they followed the process outlined in this handbook. I told the committee: "If you decide he is not your choice as the next pastor, I don't want to be involved in any of the discussion and considerations as to why he was not the choice." "If he is your choice as the next pastor, then I want you to be able to stand before the church on the Reveal Sunday and express to the church truthfully that I had no influence in the decision beyond sharing his resume with the PSC."

APPENDIX K

New Pastor Installation

[Name of Pastor], as the new pastor of **[Name of the Church, Location of the Church]**, do you pledge to give your best as shepherd, overseer, and spiritual leader? **If so, respond – I Will.**

[Name of Pastor], as the shepherd, overseer, and spiritual leader of **[Name of the Church]**, Do you promis that your priorities of ministry will be God first, family second, and church third? **If so, respond – I Will.**

[Name of Pastor, Spouse, and Children], as the new pastoral family of [Name of the Church], will you be an example of love, encouragement, and integrity to the church and community? **If so, respond – We Will.**

To the members of **[Name of the Church, Location of Church]** assembled on this day, **[Date of Installation]**, do you pledge as a congregation to love, to support, and to pray for your new pastoral family? **If so, respond – We Will.**

Do you promise to help your new pastor, not hound him; to hear him out, not hush him up; and to hug him, not hurt him? **If so, respond – We Will.**

Since the **[Name of Pastoral Family]** have accepted the pastoral responsibilities of **[Name of the Church, Location of the Church]**, it is my honor to present them to you as your new pastoral family.

Since **[Name of the Church, Location of Church]**, has received you as their new pastoral family, it is my honor to present them to you as your new church family.

Date: ________________________________

Signature: __________________________

Dr. Reggie R. Ogea, Interim Pastor

Works Cited

Books

Bauman, J. Daniel. *Introduction to Contemporary Preaching*. Grand Rapids: Baker Book House, 1972.

Bullard, Jr., George W. *Every Congregation Needs a Little Conflict*. St. Louis: Chalice Press, 2008.

Echols, Steve and Allen England, *Catastrophic Crisis: Ministry Leadership in the Midst of Trial and Tragedy*, Nashville: B & H Academic, 2011.

Hare, Michael. *When Church Conflict Happens: A Proven Process for Resolving Unhealthy Disagreements and Embracing Healthy Ones*. Chicago: Moody Press, 2019.

Hull, William E. *Strategic Preaching: The Role of the Pulpit in Pastoral Leadership*. St. Louis: Chalice Press, 2006.

Kotter, John. *A Heart of Change*. Boston: Harvard Business Review Press, 2002.

_________. *A Sense of Urgency*. Boston: Harvard Business School Publishing, 2008.

_________. *Leading Change*. Boston: Harvard Business Review Press, 1996.

_________. *Our Iceberg is Melting*. New York: St. Martin's Press, 2005.

McNeal, Reggie. *The Present Future: Six Tough Questions for the Church*. San Francisco: Jossey-Bass, 2003.

O'Hair, Dan H. and Mary John O'Hair, *Communication and Catastrophic Events: Strategic Risk and Crisis Management*, Hoboken, NJ: John Wiley and Sons, Inc., 2023.

Schaller, Lyle. *The Change Agent*. Nashville: Abingdon Press, 1972.

Websites

www.assistcx.org
www.bibletolife.com
www.churchanswers.com
www.healthychurch.net
www.interimpastors.com
www.louisianabaptists.org
www.nobts.edu

Competing Titles

Braun, Chris. *When the Word Leads Your Pastoral Search: Biblical Principles and Practices to Guide Your Search*. Chicago: Moody, 2011.
Harris, Tom. *Soaring Between Pastors: 8 Actions to Thrive During a Pastoral Transition*. Wheaton IL: Big Snowy Media, 2021.
Hunter, Ron, Jr. and David C. Gibbs III. *How to Find the Right Pastor: A Handbook for Pastoral and Staff Search Committees*. Nashville: Randall House, 2023.
Lowe, Jason. *The Church During the Search: Honoring Christ While You Wait for Your Next Pastor*. Abbotsford, WI: Aneko Press, 2020.
Transitional Pastor Ministry: Training Manual. Revised. Nashville: Lifeway Christian Resources,2014.
Utley, John. *Navigating Pastoral Transitions: A Pastoral Search Committee Handbook*. Fort Worth: Cotton House Press, 2024.
Vanderbloemen, William. *Search: The Pastor Search Committee Handbook*. Nashville: B & H Publishing Group, 2016.

www.ingramcontent.com/pod-product-compliance
Lightning Source LLC
LaVergne TN
LVHW010628100826
845148LV00014B/3154

* 9 7 9 8 2 1 8 9 4 6 1 6 6 *